GREYSTONE'S

Creative Hands

EDITOR

Beverley Hilton

GREYSTONE PRESS/NEW YORK · TORONTO · LONDON

Volume 8

Contents

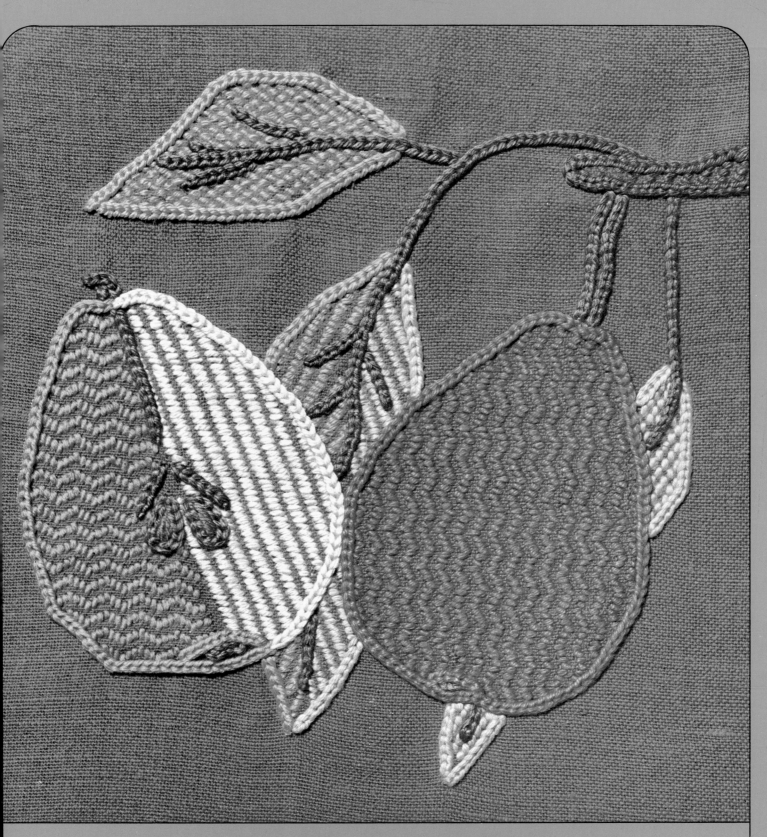

Pattern Library

A pair of pears

This pear design in brilliant colors makes interesting use of simple line stitches and filling stitches. First, the outlines and details are worked in chain stitch, and then the fillings are built up with satin stitch patterns formed into diagonal and zigzag lines. Because the satin stitch is worked by counting threads, it is essential to work on an even-weave fabric, such as linen, or a home furnishing fabric of a clearly defined weave.

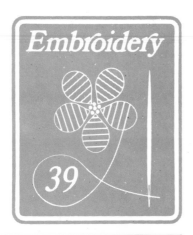

Smocking for heavier fabrics

Previous chapters on smocking have dealt with work on light-weight materials. However, it is not possible to smock satisfactorily on thick or heavy-weight fabrics such as velvet, corduroy or tweed. But a garment made of a thicker fabric can be decorated by working a panel of smocking on a matching, finer fabric—like a cotton and wool mixture such as Viyella—and inserting this into the heavier fabric.

This chapter also shows how to build up dozens of different designs from a combination of simple stitches.

Inset smocked panels

The brown velvet dress pictured here has bands of smocking worked on a finer fabric in a matching color, and an inset at waist and cuffs. When working with two weights of fabric, especially at areas such as waist and cuffs, smocking is used purely as a means of decoration. Because the heavier of the fabrics would eventually pull the smocked areas out of shape, a firm finish is required to control the elasticity of the smocking, and this is achieved by backing the area with a lining fabric. This charming little velvet dress has been treated in this way.

Working an inset

Decide where you want to place the inset band of smocking before cutting out the garment. Mark the selected area on the pattern piece and carefully cut the section out of the pattern, to use as a guide for cutting the fabric to be smocked.

Cut a length in a lighter weight fabric, three times the length of this section, adding $\frac{5}{8}$ inch seam allowance all around. When

◄ *Pretty as a picture in her brown velvet dress with smocking insets*
▼ *Chart for the stitches on the brown velvet dress smocked insets*

cutting out the rest of the garment, do not forget to add ⅝ inch seam allowance on the edges where the section was cut.

Work all smocked panels before making the garment. When they are completed, insert them into the garment by hand stitching as described in Embroidery chapter 23, page 448. Make the rest of the garment following the instructions given with the pattern.

Lining a smocked section

When a smocked section needs to be rigidly controlled, use the cutout section of the pattern to cut a lining to back the smocking, adding ⅝ inch seam allowance all around.

Once the panels have been inserted and the garment made, take the lining section and turn all seam allowances to the wrong side. Baste and press. Pin and baste the lining on the back of the smocked area, wrong sides together, and stitch the lining in place by hand. Line cuffs in the same way, binding the raw cuff edge with a bias strip cut from the heavier fabric.

Wave stitch

The panels on the brown velvet dress are a combination of wave stitch, trellis stitch and cable stitch.

Wave stitch is worked from left to right and in a similar way to cable stitch. While the upward steps are being formed, the thread lies below the needle, and when making the downward steps, it lies above the needle. The second row is worked immediately below the first.

This stitch is often repeated with the zigzag lines going in the opposite direction to create a diamond pattern.

Rows of wave stitch worked in opposite directions to form diamonds ►
▼ *An attractive design made with rows of outline stitch and crosses*

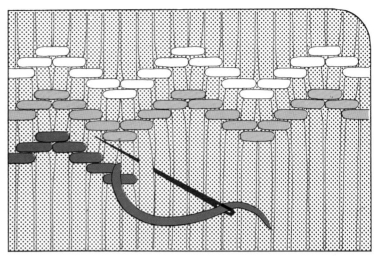

▲ *Working wave stitch*

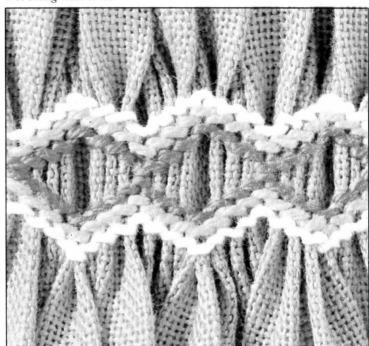

▼ *Interesting design of pyramids of double cable on single cable base*

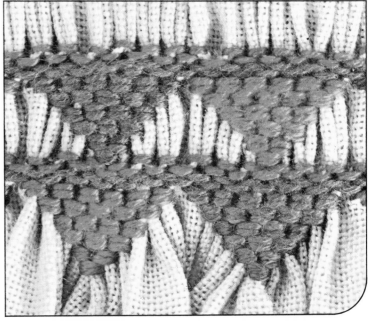

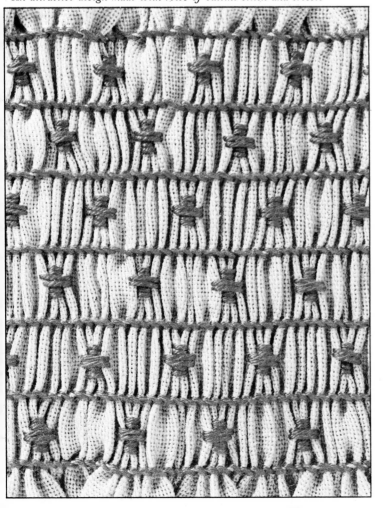

Quilted robe and matching nightgown

The garments featured here were chosen for their durability and the ease with which they are constructed.

The robe is made from a basic Butterick pattern, and the instructions given here are specially adapted for making this pattern in ready-made quilted fabric. The special techniques include marking pattern details on quilting, basting and stitching it, and making it slimming and less bulky. Even if you choose an alternative pattern, you will find these techniques applicable.

This pattern has been chosen because it is flattering and fits close to the body, so if you decide to use another one, make your choice carefully and be sure that it is not voluminous. Although a long version has been made here, this robe would look just as pretty in a short length.

The pattern comes with patch pockets which are not really suitable for quilted fabric, so there are also instructions for inserting concealed pockets into the side seams.

The robe is followed by instructions for making a nightgown in a matching fabric which is adapted from the Creative Hands basic blouse pattern.

The robe

Working with quilting

Garments made in quilted fabrics should have as little seaming as possible. The fabric is thick and seams add bulk, especially on edges, so the style should be simple.

When buying quilted fabric make sure that both fabric and fiber fill are washable. Choose a polyester fiber fill such as Fortrel or Dacron, since these have sufficient spring and will not go lumpy or flop after washing.

It is possible to buy quilted fabric with or without backing.

The instructions are for a robe which is not backed and has a separate lining. The lining should be machine stitched into the garment wherever possible.

If you buy quilting which has a backing, the garment will not require a lining.

So, to make this robe from backed quilting, follow the instructions but leave out the lining. You will need to bind seam allowances and all raw edges with matching bias binding to stop fraying or the shedding of fiber fill from between the layers. Overcasting or a zigzag finish is not strong enough to withstand many machine washings.

When machine stitching, the pressure on the presser foot must be eased. Otherwise, the work will stick under the needle or the top layer of fabric will be pushed forward while the underneath puckers up.

Use the usual sewing thread but engage a slightly larger stitch setting.

Avoid basting wherever possible because basting stitches are very difficult to remove from the fibers of the quilting. Follow the special instructions given here for marking pattern details.

Fabric and other requirements

You will need a robe pattern.

All yardages and notions are given on the pattern envelope.

For heavier quiltings, use the size 1 snap fastener, as recommended, but for finer quiltings, size 00 is more suitable.

Because the quilting fabric is firm, you will not need the interfacing given on the pattern.

The fabric for lining should be of the same type as the quilting. For instance, if you've chosen a nylon quilting use a nylon or cotton lining, and for lawn quilting use a pre-shrunk cotton lining.

The pattern

The Butterick pattern comes in sizes 8 to 18. The pattern pieces required are numbers 1, 2, 3, 4, 5 and 6.

The pattern has a well laid out instruction sheet and you can use it if you wish. But remember, those instructions have been constructed to suit a large range of fabrics, while the instructions given in this chapter are specifically for quilted fabrics. They will help eliminate bulk and achieve better results for this fabric.

Another feature of these adapted instructions is that all loose edges are enclosed between lining and quilting; this makes the garment machine washable (hand-sewn edges on top of the lining, as in the pattern instructions, should be hand-washed—they would work loose during the action of a washing machine, making frequent repair necessary).

Adapting the patterns

The front pattern piece The pattern has a separate front facing which is stitched down the front wrap on each side of the garment. This makes a thick seam along the edge which can be avoided by cutting the front and front facing in one.

To do this, lay the front pattern piece (number 1) on a table and find the stitching line on the wrap of the center front edge. Then take the front facing pattern piece (number 4) and pin the stitching line on the front edge of the facing over the stitching line of the wrap, matching all symbols, as shown (figure 1).

Ignore the step on the center front at the hem and cut the fabric straight across. Pin a piece of paper under it to remind you.

The front neck facing To avoid two seam allowances lying over each other on the shoulder dart when the facing is stitched on, move the seam in the facing forward.

To do this, cut the front neck facing as shown (figure 1), and pin the cut-off section to the back neck facing (number 5) with seam lines coinciding.

Pockets To find the position for the concealed side seam pockets, put the front pattern side seam against the side of your body and find a comfortable position for the pocket, somewhere between hip level and waistline.

Mark the pocket opening on the pattern, 6 inches long. Then mark the pattern for a double seam allowance for $7\frac{1}{4}$ inches along this edge to stitch on the pocket linings.

Also mark the corresponding position and double seam allowance on the back side seam.

To make the pattern for the pocket, first draw a straight line 6 inches long. This will be the open end and goes to the straight of the grain on the pocket lining.

To obtain the shape of the pocket, lay your open hand to the line palm down, so that the wrist below the thumb and the base of the little finger are on the line (figure 2).

Draw around your hand for the pocket shape as shown.

Before you cut out the pocket lining pattern add $\frac{5}{8}$ inch seam allowance all around.

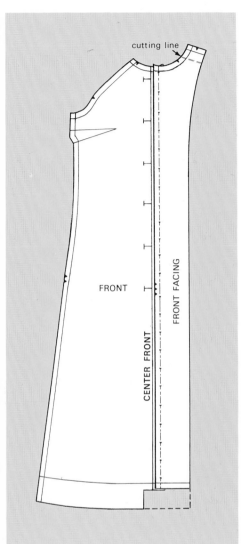

cutting line

FRONT

CENTER FRONT

FRONT FACING

1. *Joining front facing, separating neck facing Long quilted robe from a Butterick pattern*
2. *Making the pocket pattern*

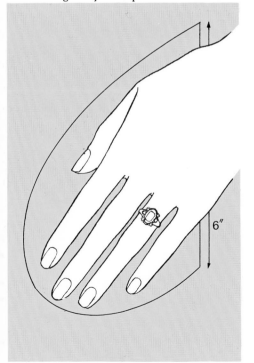

6"

Cutting out

Fold the quilted fabric right side out for cutting because the loops of the cut tailor's tacks can be removed more easily from this side.

Use the layouts on the instruction sheet as your cutting guide. If you have made the Creative Hands pattern adaptations you may have to cut some sizes on an open layout to accommodate the extended front pattern.

Remember to add seam allowances where neck and front facings were separated.

Reduce the hem allowance to 2 inches, as deep hems on quilted fabrics tend to roll downward and need frequent repair.

Cut out the robe.

The pockets are cut from the lining later.

Marking the pattern detail

To tailor's tack the darts and pattern details other than the seamlines, work single tailor's tacks through slits in the pattern. Mark the seamlines with colored chalk similar to the color of the fabric.

To do this, first pin the pattern pieces to the fabric along the seamlines, catching both layers in the pins. Unpin the seam allowance to get to the wrong side of the fabric and make a chalk mark over each pin where you can feel it or see it between the layers.

To mark the fold line for the facing on the center front wrap, which is where the pattern seamlines are pinned over each other, make slits through both layers of paper and mark with single tailor's tacks. Mark all symbols for matching.

Preparing for fitting

Remove the pattern and carefully separate the layers.

Fold the front facing under along the fold line. Pin and baste in place.

Pin and baste the center back seam, the side bust darts and the side seams.

Pin and baste the darts on the shoulder of each raglan sleeve.

Pin and baste the sleeve seams, then baste the sleeves into the armholes.

Fit the robe and make any necessary alterations.

Making the robe

After you have made all the fitting corrections, remove the sleeves and take out all the basting which is holding the seams and darts together.

Repin the side bust darts and, beside the seamline, make a fresh row of basting stitches so that they cannot be caught up in the machine stitches. Because the thickness of the quilting will make them tilt toward the needle, the basting stitches must be at least $\frac{1}{4}$ inch away from the

stitching line. Stitch the darts.

Leave the pins in the seamlines to serve as a guide, removing each pin just before the needle reaches it. All the seams and darts are stitched in the same way.

This is a useful exercise, because as you gain more dressmaking experience you will want to stitch pinned seams, as well as basted ones, to save time.

Remove the basting, slash the darts along the center and press open.

Pin and baste the center back and the side seams, leaving the pocket openings. Stitch, using the chalk line markings for the seamlines.

Remove basting and press all seams open. Press quilting as you would other man-made fiber fabrics, but do not use steam or a damp cloth because this would flatten the quilted fabric.

Stitch, remove the basting and press the sleeve darts and seams open. Stitch the sleeves into armholes, matching symbols. Remove the basting and press the armhole seams in two stages.

First press them open from the neck edge down, as far as the seam allowance will let you without it straining into the sleeves. Then press the rest of the seam, around the lower armhole edge, into the sleeve. Do not cut the seam allowance at the transition point as this would weaken the armhole seam.

Stitching the facing and collar

To make the facing in one piece along the front and neck edge of the garment, pin, baste and stitch the neck facing between the front facings where you separated the pattern. Press the seams open. Make the mandarin collar following the pattern instructions (Robe A, step 6) but do not use the interfacing.

The quilted collar is attached in a different way from that given in the instructions; it is caught in the seam when the neck facing is stitched on.

So baste the raw edges of the collar together and pin it to the neckline on the outside of the garment, matching all symbols.

Turn the whole facing to the outside of the garment, right sides together, and pin and baste the neck facing to the neckline, catching the collar between facing and garment.

Make sure that the front facings are folded on the foldline markings and have not moved, then stitch all layers of fabric together along the neck edge.

Trim and snip into the seam allowance and turn the facing to the inside again. Edge baste the neckline and press.

Baste the front facing close to the fold and press the edges.

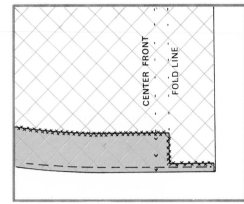

▲ 3. *Trimming the front facing at the hem*
▼ 4. *Placing front and sleeve patterns together*

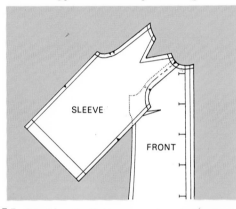

▼ 5. *Marking the lining seam edges on the front*

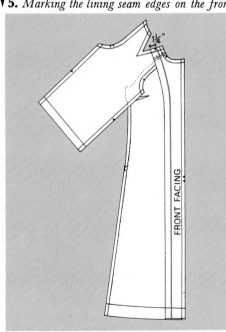

Making the hems

Turn up the sleeve hems and sew them to the sleeves with catch stitches.

Rip the basting at the hem of the front facing. Open out the facing and turn up the hem. Baste in place close to the hemline.

To avoid the thickness of two layers of hem allowance when the facing is stitched over the hem, cut out some of the fabric on the facing hem allowance.

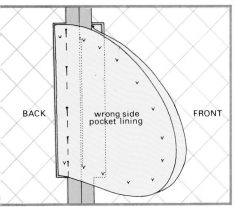

▲ 6. *Pinning pocket pieces to double allowance*

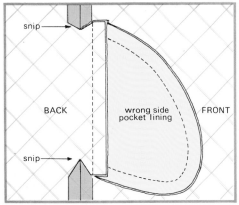

▲ 7. *Snipping the back seam allowance*

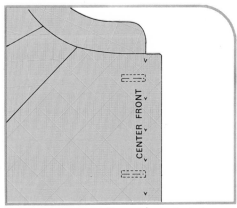

▲ 8. *Stitching the outlines of the buttonholes*

Cut along the fold line as shown (figure **3**) leaving ½ inch hem allowance only on the facing.
The hem edges should be finished with catch stitches.
Do not stitch the facing to the hem yet.

The lining pattern pieces
You will need pattern piece numbers 1, 2 and 3, and your own pocket pattern for cutting out the lining.

Adapting the lining pattern
To cut the lining so that it can be machine stitched into the robe the pattern needs to be prepared first. You will need a large surface to work on.
Unpin the front facing from the front pattern, and the front neck facing from the back neck facing.
Join the cut-off section of the front neck facing to the front facing again, with the edges meeting over a strip of paper.
Pin the sleeve and front pattern pieces together along the front armhole seam for 2 to 3 inches, starting at the neck edge (figure **4**). Do not pin the sleeve dart together and make sure that the pattern pieces remain perfectly flat.
Position the complete front facing pattern piece over the front and sleeve pattern pieces as shown (figure **5**).
Measure out a line 1¼ inches (a double seam allowance) in from the solid line of the facing pattern, which is the inner edge of the facing, and trace the line with a tracing wheel through both layers of pattern (see the red line in figure **5**).
Unpin the facing, sleeve and front pattern pieces.
Pin the back sleeve pattern to the back armhole seam and the back neck facing over the neckline edge of the sleeve and back pattern pieces in the same manner. Again, mark out a line 1¼ inches in from the inner facing edge with a tracing wheel.
Unpin the pattern pieces.
These traced lines are the cutting lines for the lining. Do not cut the pattern along

these lines, but use the tracing wheel to mark them on the fabric. The perforations will be lost when the fabric is cut along them.
Pin up the hem allowances on the front, back and sleeve pattern pieces.

Cutting out the lining
Place the pattern pieces on the lining fabric, following the layout on the instruction sheet. Place the pattern for the pocket linings where there is a space—you will need two pieces for each pocket.
Cut out the lining.
Trace the front and neck cutting lines through the pattern and cut along these lines, lifting the pattern out of the way of the scissors.

Making the linings
Stitch the seams and darts. Press the darts toward the hem and press all the long seams open.
The lining armhole seams should be pressed in the same way as those on the quilted fabric.

Stitching in the lining
The pocket lining Pin the straight edge of a pocket lining piece to each double seam allowance at the pocket openings, with right sides facing and pockets pointing downward as shown (figure **6**).
Stitch, taking ⅝ inch seams, and press the seams open.
Now stitch the pocket linings together to form the pocket. Fold the side seam so that both pocket lining pieces are together with raw edges level and stitch.
Snip the side seam allowance on the back only as shown and press the pockets toward the front (figure **7**).
The garment lining Make ½ inch snips into the back neck curve of the lining, then pin the lining to the facing as follows.
Turn the facing to the right side of the garment again. On the inner facing edge, mark the positions where the facing falls on the armhole seams.

Put the right side of the lining over the right side of the robe. Pin and baste the lining to the loose facing edge, right sides facing, center backs and armhole seam positions matching.
Although you cut a double seam allowance on this edge of the lining, take only one seam allowance on the lining and one on the facing edge. Stitch the lining to the facing, leaving 4 inches unstitched above the hem on both sides.
Slip the lining over a sleeveboard so that you can reach all sections of the long seam, and press the seam into the lining.
Turn the lining and facing to the inside of the garment.
Sew the seam allowances of the lining to the seam allowances of the garment wherever you can, using small basting stitches. This will prevent the seam allowances from turning when the garment is washed.
Stitch the lining to the sleeve hem with small, firm slip stitches.
Fold the facing over the hem on the front edges and sew down by hand, then sew the lining over the hem of the garment.

Buttonholes
Mark the buttonhole sizes in the positions shown on the pattern.
Both hand-sewn and machine-stitched buttonholes can be worked successfully on quilted fabrics. If you make them by machine, just follow the instructions in your machine manual.
If you want to work them by hand, first machine stitch the outline of the buttonhole with an ordinary straight stitch (figure **8**). This will stop the thick layers of fabric moving after they have been cut.

Finishing
Stitch the buttons opposite the buttonholes and fasten the top corner of the center front wrap with a snap fastener.
If you want to make a belt, use pattern piece number 10, and follow the instructions for making Robe C, step 2.

Make a matching nightgown

Many shops sell the same fabric both with and without quilting, so you can make a perfectly matching nightgown.

For this nightgown you do not need a pattern. The front and back of the basic blouse from the Creative Hands Pattern Pack given in Volume 22 are used to shape the armholes, and the rest is cut out by simple measurements.

Fabric requirements and notions

☐ Fabric: 36 inches wide or wider. For sizes up to a 40 inch hip (or 40 inch bust), the yardage required is twice the length from neck to hem; for larger sizes allow an extra 10 inches.

☐ Ribbon to make a tie belt

☐ Lace trimming (optional)

☐ Matching thread

Calculating width for back and front

Take your bust or hip measurement, whichever is the larger, and then add on half the total measurement.

The back and front will be cut on a fabric fold, so divide this measurement by four. To proportion the back and front properly, add 1 inch to the front measurement and subtract 1 inch from the back.

Preparing the fabric and cutting

Divide the length of the fabric in half and mark with a pin line across the whole width. If you are working on a size larger than a 40 inch hip (or bust), first cut off the extra 10 inches before folding.

Both front and back sections are cut on the lengthwise fold of the fabric, so fold over the fabric to accommodate the front section plus seam allowance exactly, and cut out from the top half of the fabric. Then refold the bottom half to accommodate the back plus seam allowance exactly and cut out.

Cutting out this way means that for sizes up to a 40 inch hip (or bust) you have a continuous remnant down the side from which the bands and straps will be cut. Larger sizes will use the extra 10 inches for this.

Using the blouse pattern

First stitch the back and front nightgown sections together to form a tube. Make French seams and press them toward the front.

Take the back and front blouse pattern pieces and lay a triangle to the center front and center back so that you can draw a straight line across the pattern, in line with the lowest point of the armhole (figure 9).

To find the correct armhole depth, draw another line 2 inches above and parallel to the first. Turn the top section of each pattern piece under on this line and pin.

Fold the stitched fabric seam to seam and raw edges even (figure **10**). Pin the layers together firmly, then pin the back and front blouse pattern pieces to the seam-line as shown.

Cut the armhole close to the pattern edge and do not leave a seam allowance.

Remove the pattern pieces and unpin the top sections.

Cutting the back and front bands

Measure the back and front blouse pattern pieces along the upper straight line. Double each measurement (your pattern is only a half pattern) and add ½ inch seam allowance at each end.

Cut strips of fabric from the remnant, 5 inches wide and to the length of each measurement plus seam allowance, for the back and the front.

Cutting the shoulder straps

To find the length of the shoulder straps, place the blouse back and front pattern pieces together as shown (figure **11**) and measure the length of the armhole between the upper straight lines. Add 1 inches at each end for seam allowance and tapering.

Cut two strips of fabric 5 inches wide to the length of the measurement.

Armhole binding

To bind the armhole edges, cut a bias strip to the length of each armhole. Cut them 1 to 1¼ inches wide, depending on the fabric so that the finished rouleau-type binding will be ¼ inch wide.

Making the nightgown

The back and front With the back and front still pinned at the sideseams, mark the center back and center front along the folds. Unpin.

Bind the armhole edges with the bias strips as shown for the girl's dress in Dressmaking chapter 25, page 496. Leave the ends of the binding open as they will be caught in the bands.

Make a double row of gathering stitches along the top front and back edges between the armholes. Draw up the gathers to fit the measurement of the upper straight line on the corresponding blouse pattern piece.

Secure the gathering threads by winding around a pin.

The straps Fold each strap in half lengthwise, right sides facing, and stitch the long edge taking ½ inch seam allowance. Press the seam open.

Turn to the right side and press so that the seam goes to the center of the back of the straps (see tie belt, Dressmaking chapter 12, page 236).

Pin both straps together with outsides facing each other, and taper each end for about ½ inch as shown (figure **12**).

The shorter side is the armhole edge.

Working from the inside of the nightgown,

▼9. *Finding armhole depth on the blouse pattern*

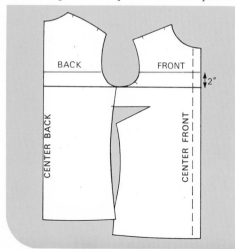

▼10. *Marking armholes on folded fabric*

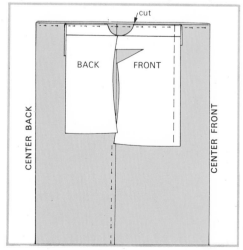

▼11. *Measuring for the shoulder strap length*

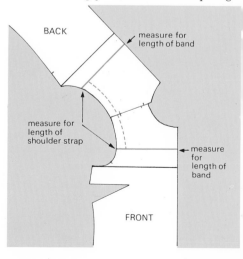

pin the straps to the gathered edge, wrong sides facing, with the armhole edge of the straps $\frac{1}{2}$ inch in from the armhole edge of the nightgown, and raw edges even. Baste firmly in position.

The bands Mark the center front and center back on each band. Working on the outside of the nightgown, pin and baste the bands to the gathered edge, with right sides facing, raw edges even, and leaving $\frac{1}{2}$ inch seam allowance over the armhole edge on each side.

Before stitching the bands, try on the nightgown and check the fitting on the shoulders. Stitch the bands in position and press the seams into the bands.

Fold in the seam allowance along the long raw edge of each band and baste. Also turn in seam allowances at each end.

Pin and baste the folded edge over the seamline on the wrong side to cover the raw seam edges.

Using a small, firm slip stitch, sew the ends together and sew the folded edge in place.

Sew the bands to the shoulder straps to hold them up.

Turn up the hem on the nightgown and stitch by hand or machine.

Trimming

There are many ways to trim and finish this nightgown so that you can have a number of variations, both long and short, based on this one design, yet each looking different.

You can sew on lace and frills or make the shoulder straps and bands in contrasting fabric or lace.

Although the nightgown featured here is belted with a ribbon you can make a casing for elastic or a ribbon tie, or use a slotted ribbon lace, which can be drawn up and positioned just under the bust or at waist level.

Make a nightgown to match the quilted robe ►
▼ **12.** *Tapering the ends of the straps*

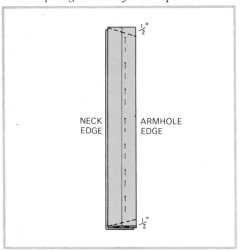

NECK EDGE   ARMHOLE EDGE

Make yours a tote bag

Needlepoint is ideal for making all kinds of bags, from elegant evening purses worked in fine silk to casual hold-alls in colorful wool. By following the chart on page 782 you can make this richly decorated tote bag, which is worked in tapestry yarn with touches of plastic raffia—a beautiful and practical present for a friend.

Tote bag

Materials you will need to work both sides of the bag
- [ ] ½yd single-weave canvas 36in wide, 18 threads to 1 inch
- [ ] ½yd lining material, 36in wide
- [ ] Two skeins each of D.M.C. Tapestry yarn in dark blue No. 7319, blue No. 7996, green No. 7344, pink No. 7153, turquoise No. 7912, lime green No. 7435; four skeins pale blue No. 7604; twenty skeins purple No. 7245
- [ ] Two skeins Straw Yarn purple
- [ ] Tapestry needle No. 18

To use the pattern
Draw the outline of the bag from the chart onto strong paper and cut out. Baste the pattern onto the canvas, leaving plenty of space around the shape for $\frac{5}{8}$ inch seam allowance and blocking. Also make sure that the grain line on the pattern follows the grain of the canvas.

Draw around the outline of the pattern using a felt-tipped pen, or mark with basting stitches. Remove the pattern and repeat the process for the other side of the bag.

Or you could work only one side of the bag in canvas, using a textured fabric such as tweed for the second side, halving the amounts of yarn required.

To work the embroidery
Mark the center of each side with lines of basting (Needlepoint chapter 9, page 272) and plan how to work the design out from the center. Using the chart, work the design on each side of the bag.

To make the bag
When the work is complete block and trim the canvas (Needlepoint chapter 5, page 112) and cut out the two pieces of lining to the shape of the trimmed canvas.

Pin and baste the two sides of the bag together, right sides facing, stitch from A to B (see diagram) using one of the seaming methods given, then stitch the seam of the handle (see diagram).

Snip into the seam allowance on curves, and turn the bag to the right side. Fold back the seam allowance around the upper edge of the bag and handle edges and baste down.

Sew the pieces of lining together in the same way as for the bag, folding the seam allowance around the top and along the handle to the back, and baste. Slip the lining into the bag, matching the

seams to those of the bag. Pin, baste, and slip stitch into place, taking care to bring the lining right up to the edge of the embroidery so that no canvas is visible on the finished bag.

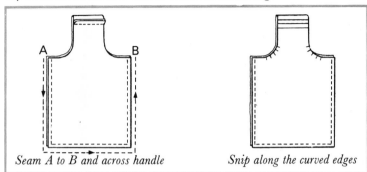

Seam A to B and across handle   *Snip along the curved edges*

Seam methods
For needlepoint items which receive hard wear, a good strong method of seaming is needed.

After blocking the finished work (Needlepoint chapter 5, page 112) trim away excess canvas leaving not less than $\frac{5}{8}$ inch seam allowance all around. Place the work with right sides together and pin, matching any patterns carefully, and then baste. Backstitch by hand using either yarn of the background color or matching linen thread. If you prefer to machine stitch the seam, use a strong linen thread matched to the background color. Stitches should be placed as close as possible to the edge of the embroidery.

Overcast the raw edges of canvas to prevent fraying and trim back the corners. Turn the work to the right side and if any canvas shows along the seams, work a slip stitch, picking up one stitch of embroidery from each side of the seam to draw the stitches together over the canvas.

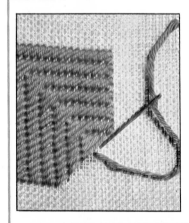

Satin stitch
These blocked rows of satin stitch show the method used for turning a corner.

Finally, here is one more stitch to add to your needlepoint repertoire. This stitch produces a damask-like texture which will add richness to your work. It can be used either to highlight areas of a design or as a background stitch.

▼ *Close-up of textured stitches used on the tote bag pictured opposite*

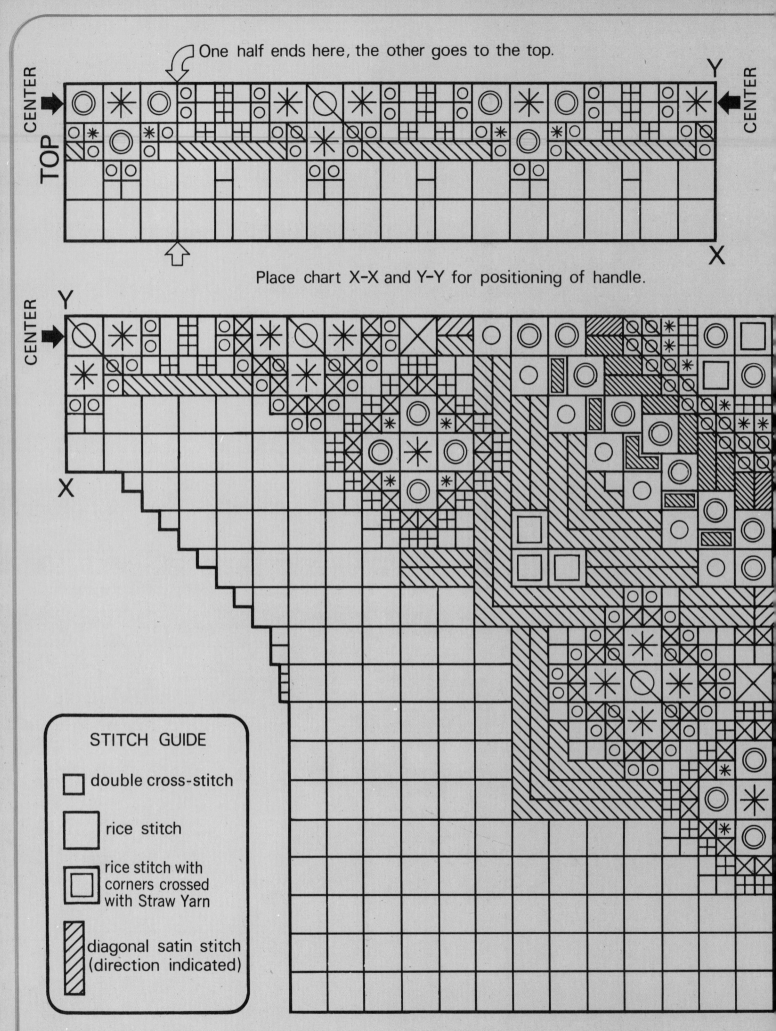

One half ends here, the other goes to the top.

CENTER → TOP ← CENTER

Y

CENTER

X

Place chart X–X and Y–Y for positioning of handle.

Y

CENTER

X

STITCH GUIDE

☐ double cross-stitch

☐ rice stitch

▣ rice stitch with corners crossed with Straw Yarn

▨ diagonal satin stitch (direction indicated)

Working chart for the tote bag

D.M.C. TAPESTRY YARN COLOR CHART

⊡ = pink _____ 7153

⊠ = dark blue _____ 7319

◎ = blue _____ 7996

⊘ = turquoise _____ 7912

▨ ✳ = green _____ 7344

⊞ = pale blue _____ 7604

▨ = lime _____ 7435

☐ = purple _____ 7245

purple-Straw Yarn

Double cross-stitch worked over 2 threads each way.
Other stitches worked in proportion to this stitch.

← CENTER

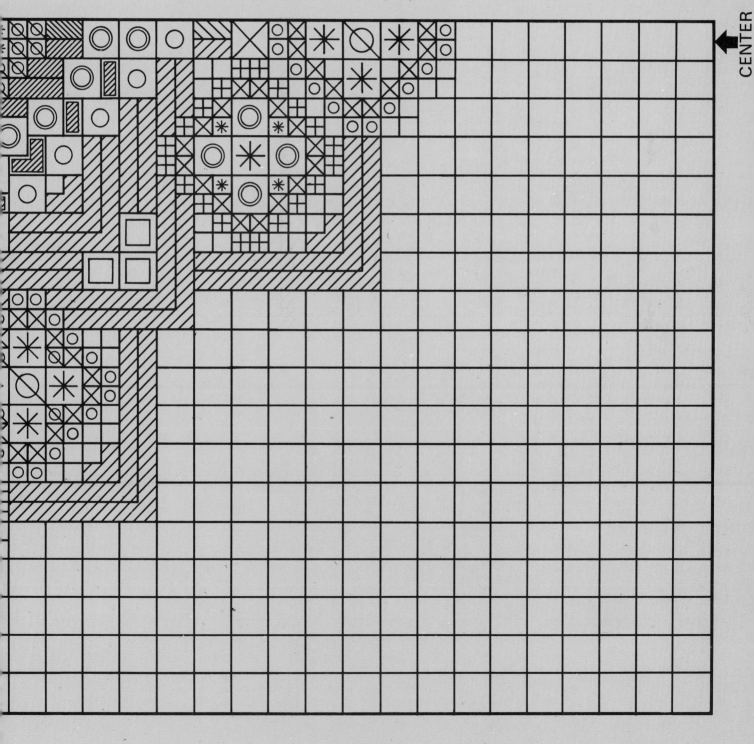

After-dark glamour in crochet

Make this elegant long dress, crocheted in a simple stitch which has a see-through look without being too open, for glamorous evenings of wining and dining. Wear it over trousers or as it is.

Sizes
Directions are for 34-36in bust with 36-38in hips. Length down center back, 57in. Sleeve seam, 17½in.

> **Gauge**
> 6 stitches and 3 rows to one inch worked over pattern on No.E crochet hook.

Materials
Reynolds Parfait
32 30 gram skeins
One No.E (3.50 mm) crochet hook
6in zipper

Back
Using No.E crochet hook, ch138.
1st row 1dc into 3rd ch from hook, 1dc into each ch to end. Turn. 136 sts.
2nd row Ch5, *skip 2dc, 1dc into next dc, ch2, rep from * to end, working 1dc into turning ch. Turn.
3rd row Ch5, *1dc into next dc, (2dc into ch2 sp, 1dc into next dc) 3 times, ch2, rep from * to end, working 1dc into turning ch. Turn.
4th row Ch5, *1dc into each of next 4dc, ch2, skip 2dc, 1dc into each of next 4dc, ch2, rep from * to end, working 1dc into turning ch. Turn.
5th row Ch5, *1dc into each of next 4dc, 2dc into ch2 sp, 1dc into each of next 4dc, ch2, rep from * to end, working 1dc into turning ch. Turn.
6th row Ch5, *1dc into next dc, (ch2, skip 2dc, 1dc into next dc) 3 times, ch2, rep from * to end, working 1dc into turning ch. Turn.
Rep rows 3-6 inclusive 14 times more—62 rows in all. Work should then measure approximately 20½in from beg.

Make side slits
Next row Ch5, 1dc into 1st and 2nd of these 5ch, 1dc into turning ch dc of previous row, ch2, 1dc into next dc, patt to end.
Next row As last row. 142 sts.
Continue in patt, dec one st at each end of every 4th row until 112 sts rem.
Continue without shaping until work measures 50in from beg, or desired length to underarm.

Shape armholes
Next row Ss over first 6 sts, patt to last 6 sts, turn.
Dec one st at each end of next 6 rows. 88 sts.
Continue without shaping until armholes measure 3in from beg.

Divide for back opening
Next row Patt over first 43 sts, turn.
Continue in patt until armhole measures 7in from beg, ending at center edge.

Shape shoulder
Next row Patt to last 8 sts, turn.
Next row Ss over first 8 sts, patt next 8 sts. Fasten off.
With RS of work facing, skip next 2 sts for center back, attach yarn to rem sts and patt to end. Complete to match first side.

Front
Work as given for Back until armhole shaping is completed. Continue without shaping until armholes measure 5 rows less than Back.

Shape neck
Next row Patt over first 35 sts, turn.
Next row Ss over first 3 sts, patt to end, turn.
Next row Patt to last 3 sts, turn.
Next row Ss over first 3 sts, patt to end, turn.
Next row Patt to last 2 sts, turn.
Next row Patt to last 8 sts, turn.
Next row Ss over first 8 sts, patt to end. Fasten off.
With RS of work facing, skip next 18 sts for center neck, attach yarn to rem sts and patt to end. Complete to match first side.

Sleeves
Using No.E crochet hook, Ch54.
Work in patt as given for Back (52 sts) for 6 rows.
Continue in patt, inc one st at each end of next and every following 4th row until there are 76 sts.
Continue without shaping until sleeve measures 17½in from beg, or desired length to underarm.

Shape cap
Next row Ss over first 6 sts, patt to last 6 sts, turn.
Dec one st at each end of next 6 rows.
Next row Patt to last 4 sts, turn.
Rep last row 9 times more. Finish off.

Finishing
Press each piece under a damp cloth with a warm iron. Join shoulder and sleeve seams. Join side seams as far as side slits.
Collar. Using No.E crochet hook, ch90. Work in patt as given for Back (88sts) for 10 rows. Finish off.
Slit edges. Using No.E crochet hook and with RS of work facing, attach yarn to lower edge and work 1 row of dc to where extra sts were cast on, working 2dc into each row. Finish off.
Sew in sleeves. Sew on collar. Work 2 rows sc along sides of collar and back opening. Sew in zipper. Press seams.

Cord belt
Using No.E crochet hook and yarn double throughout, ch2. Insert hook into first ch, *yoh, draw through a loop yoh, draw through both loops on hook*, insert hook into the left of these 2 loops and work from * to * for required length. Finish off

▼ *Stitch detail*

Dress with a metal link belt ▶

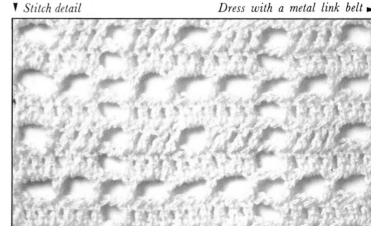

Mitered corners and 'V'necks

Although most crochet patterns give detailed directions, it is helpful to know how shaping is worked, particularly when adapting a favorite design to crochet. Previous chapters tell you how to choose the right stitch for a garment and all about gauge. This chapter gives directions for working a pointed and a rounded mitered corner, sleeve underarm shaping and V-necklines.

This charming crochet two-piece dress shows the effective use of V-neck shaping, which is defined by an edging in a single contrasting color. The contrasting color theme is continued at the hem in a single color and in two colors above cuff level on the sleeves of the slim fitting top.

The skirt is worked in bands of all three colors, from side edge to side edge to give a vertical striped effect, and the whole ensemble has an air of elegance and distinction.

Pointed mitered corner

To make a separate band having a pointed mitered corner, first measure the length of band required and make the necessary number of chains. Mark the stitch which is to be the innermost point of the corner with colored thread. The band is worked from the inside to the outside edge.

1st row (right side). Work 1sc into 2nd ch from hook, then work 1sc into each ch to the last ch before the marked corner ch, ch2 and continue working 1sc into each ch to end. Turn.

2nd row. Ch2, work 1sc into each sc and 1sc into each of the 2ch at corner. Turn.

Continue in this way, working 2ch at corner on every RS row working 1 more sc on each RS row before making the 2ch and working 1sc into each of these 2ch on WS rows until the band is the required depth. Fasten off.

Any number of chains may precede and follow the corner stitches, depending on the angle of the corner, but always

work one more stitch before corner chain on each RS row.

Rounded mitered corner

Prepare the band as for pointed mitered corner.

1st row (right side). Work 1sc into 2nd ch from hook, then 1sc into each ch to marked corner st, work 3sc into corner st and 1sc into each ch to end. Turn.

2nd row. Ch2, work 1sc into each sc to end. Turn. Repeat these 2 rows until band is the required depth, working 3sc into center stitch of the 3 corner stitches on each RS row.

Sleeve underarm shaping

To give a good underarm fit, the same number of stitches should be decreased on the back and front of a garment and at the commencement of the sleeve cap shaping. Work until the back and front side seams and the sleeve seam are the required length.

1st row. Ss over first 5 sts, work 1sc into each sc to last 5 sts. Turn.

2nd row. Ch2, skip 1sc, work 1sc into each sc to last 2sc, skip 1sc, work 1sc into last sc. Turn.

Repeat the 2nd row for a depth of 1½in. Fasten off.

V-neckline

The depth of the V-neck is entirely a matter of choice, but keep in mind that the deeper the "V," the more gradual the shaping, and that a high "V" must decrease more rapidly in order to complete the shaping before reaching the shoulder level. On a 34in bust size an average depth for a V-neck is approximately 10in from the shoulder, which means that the shaping must be commenced at least 3in before the armhole shaping. Mark the position of the center stitch and work each side separately.

1st row (right side). Ch2, work 1sc into each sc, skip 1sc before marked center st, work 1sc into center st. Turn.

2nd row. Ch2, work in sc to end. Rep 2nd row twice more.

5th row. Ch2, work 1sc into each sc, skip last sc but one at

▲ *Pointed mitered corner*

▲ *Rounded mitered corner*

▲ *Sleeve underarm shaping*

▼ *V-neck shaping*

neck edge, work 1sc into last sc. Turn.

Repeat rows 2-5 until required number of stitches have been decreased at neck edge, then continue without shaping, if necessary, to a depth of 10in.

With RS of work facing, attach yarn to center st.

1st row. Ch2, skip 1sc, work 1sc into each sc to end. Turn. Work 3 rows without shaping.

Repeat these 4 rows to match first side.

An alternative method of shaping may be worked as follows:

1st row (right side). Ch2, work 1sc into each sc to last 2 sts before center st, insert hook into next sc, yoh and draw loop through, insert hook in last sc, yoh and draw loop through (3 loops on hook),

yoh and draw through all loops in hook (1 dec made), work 1sc into center st. Turn.

Work 3 rows without shaping.

5th row. Ch2, work 1sc into each sc to last 3sc, 1 dec in next 2sc, 1sc in last sc. Turn.

Repeat rows 2-5 until required number of stitches have been decreased at neck edge, then continue without shaping, if necessary, to a depth of 10in.

With RS of work facing, attach yarn to center st.

1st row. Ch2, insert hook in next st, yoh, draw loop through, insert hook in next st, yoh and draw loop through, yoh and draw through 3 loops on hook, work 1sc into each sc to end. Turn. Work 3 rows without shaping.

Repeat these 4 rows to match first side.

Dress pattern to smock for 6-10 year olds

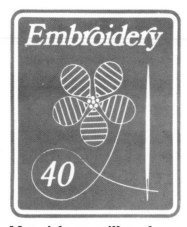

Embroidery

40

It should only take a few evenings to complete this charming child's dress with its pretty smocked collar and cuffs. It is made in a crisp, fresh gingham so that the small checks can be used as a guide for working the smocking panels. The same pattern will also make a lovely little nightgown.

Measurements
To fit a size 6-8 (9-10) year old

Materials you will need
Short-sleeved version
- [ ] 1½ (2)yd small check 36in gingham (¾ inch across each square)

Long-sleeved version
- [ ] 1¾ (2¼)yd gingham

Both versions
- [ ] 1 ball orange pearl cotton No.8
- [ ] 1 ball white pearl cotton No.8
- [ ] Snap fasteners or small buttons for back fastening

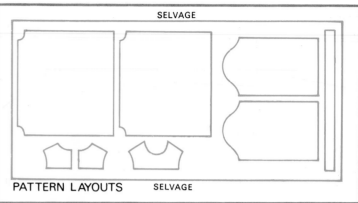

SELVAGE

PATTERN LAYOUTS   SELVAGE

▼ *Size 6-8 years, long sleeves*   ▲ *Size 9-10 years, long sleeves*

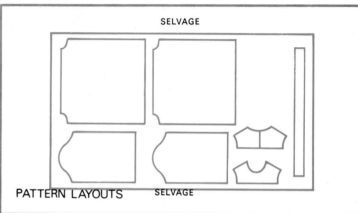

SELVAGE

PATTERN LAYOUTS   SELVAGE

▼ *Red: size 6-8 years; blue: size 9-10 years*

▼ *Detail shows effect of working three patterns for a deeper panel*

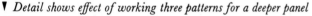

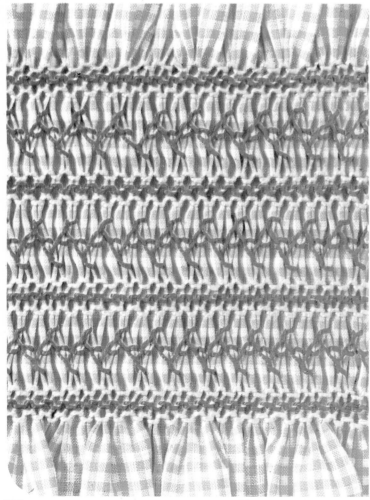

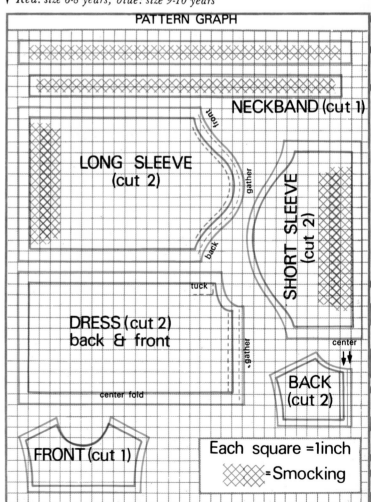

PATTERN GRAPH

NECKBAND (cut 1)

LONG SLEEVE (cut 2)

front

gather

back

SHORT SLEEVE (cut 2)

tuck

DRESS (cut 2) back & front

gather

center

center fold

BACK (cut 2)

FRONT (cut 1)

Each square =1inch

⊠ =Smocking

To make the pattern

Mark up a large sheet of brown paper in 1 inch squares and copy the pattern graph onto it, square by square. Cut out the pattern pieces.

To cut out

When cutting out the dress, allow $\frac{5}{8}$ inch seam allowances and 4 inches for the hem. Lay the material flat and pin the pattern pieces to it as shown in the pattern layout.

To make the dress

Make a small hem at the top of the neckband and at each end of it, either by hand or machine. Gather the smocking bands on the collar and sleeves by picking up the white squares on the wrong side of the work. Pull up the threads quite tightly so that the right side of the work is firm and evenly pleated. Smock three rows of cable stitch, one of feather stitch, three of cable stitch, one of feather stitch and three of cable stitch (see detail) on neck and sleeves.

Join the shoulder seams of Front and Back yokes. Cut a 4 inch opening down the Center Back of skirt top. Gather the top of the skirt to measure the same as across yokes. Join the side seams, then mark one inch out to either side of the seam and bring these two points together over the seam to make a pleat. Turn the pleat to the Front of the dress (see diagram).

Slip stitch the neckband by hand to the neck of the yoke, picking up each tube separately, leaving seam allowance plus $\frac{3}{4}$ inch at the back of the yoke to be hemmed for opening. Machine stitch around edge of yoke to secure the neckband turning. Hem neck opening as in diagram and finish with snaps or tiny buttons, making buttonhole loops to fasten. Stitch the sleeve seam, then gather around the top of the sleeve to fit the armhole and set the sleeves into armholes. Make a narrow hem on sleeve cuffs. Overcast all raw edges or finish with machine zigzagging. Turn up hem.

▲ *No worries about washing her dress, made of small check gingham and decorated with pretty panels of smocking*

▼ *Making a pleat in the side seam*   ▼ *Basting the neckband to the yoke*   ▼ *A detail of the back opening*

 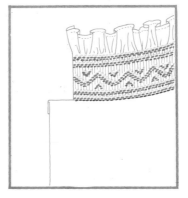 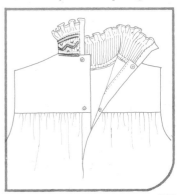

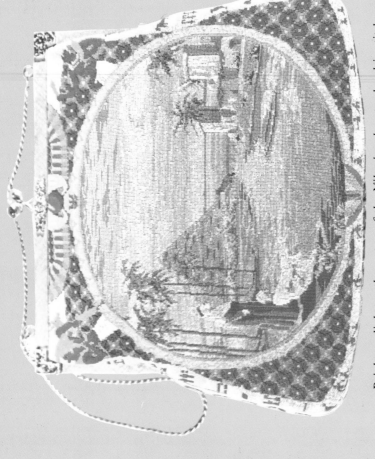

Bright sunlight on the waters of the Nile cleverly reproduced in stitches

The Fête Champêtre, an open-air festivity styled on peasant revels, enjoyed by the nobility

Collector's Piece

Petit Point Bags

These French-style bags are based on an eighteenth century design and, unlike the mass-produced versions which are woven by machine, each of them has been worked with wool in petit point by hand.

It is easy to tell the difference, for on machine-made bags each row has a smooth, corded look, while genuine hand-made stitches are clearly separate.

Petit point is worked in fine wool, silk or cotton on single-weave canvas—20 stitches to the inch mesh or smaller. Worked in pure silk, there can be as many as 30 petit point stitches to the inch. The scenes depicted on the bags were probably inspired by, or copied from, paintings, and the two pastoral scenes show the strong contrast of colors used to convey light and shade. Notice, for example, the folds of material in the ladies' dresses, and the ripples on the surface of the pond.

The bag bearing an Egyptian scene is framed by small red figures and geometrical patterns of red, blue and white. This border accentuates the simplicity of the picture, with its wide expanses of river and sky.

The firmness and durability of petit point make it particularly suitable for fashion accessories such as bags and belts, and also for larger items like chair covers.

791

Round tables - the full treatment

Home Sewing 10

Space saving and charming, round tables look attractive in both traditional and modern decors. This chapter gives instructions for making tablecloths for them.

Suitable fabrics
Easily washable dress or home furnishing fabrics such as cotton, linen, man-made fiber mixtures and cotton lace are all suitable for tablecloths. Vinyl may not hang as well as a softer fabric, but it is spongeable and would be fine for a child's room or kitchen table. Sheeting is also available now in a variety of colors, and is particularly suitable because of its quality and width.

Measuring for the cloth
The cloth will cover the table and hang down all around. The depth to which the cloth hangs is a matter of personal choice, but a deep overhang tends to make the cloth look better.
To decide the depth of the overhang, lay a tape measure across the table and let one end drop down until it looks right (figure 1). Multiply the measurement of the overhang by two.

▼ 1. *Measuring for the overhang*

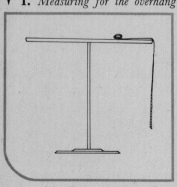

Then measure the diameter of the table, add this measurement to the doubled depth of the overhang and add 1 inch for turnings. An example is given here for a 3ft 6in table with a chosen overhang of 1ft 5in.

Overhang		
(1ft 5in × 2)	= 2ft	10in
Table diameter	= 3ft	6in
Turnings	=	1in
Cloth diameter	= 6ft	5in

The final measurement is the most important when buying fabric, but if you draw a little diagram with all the measurements marked on it (figure 2), it will also help you when you make the pattern for the cloth.

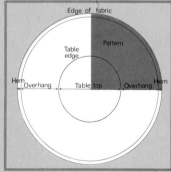

▲ 2. *The vital statistics*

Fabric widths
A circular tablecloth is made from a square of fabric, each side of the square having the same length as the diameter of the tablecloth.
Home furnishing fabrics are usually sold in 48in widths, but it is possible to buy them wider. Dress fabrics, or those which

are most suitable for tablecloths, come in differing widths from 36in to 60in.
Sheeting is usually very wide and varies in width from 35in to 90in for unbleached (which you can dye), and is 81in wide for colored sheeting. It is, of course, possible to make a round tablecloth from a patterned double sheet so long as the diameter of the cloth does not exceed the width of the sheet.
If the width of the fabric you choose is less than the diameter of the tablecloth, it will be necessary to join more fabric to the sides of the main piece. It will help you when calculating yardage to remember that the main piece and any extra side pieces must be the same length as the diameter of the tablecloth, and the joined widths must also be equal to the diameter.

Making the pattern

You will need
☐ A square of brown wrapping paper, with each side a little longer than the radius (or half the diameter) of the tablecloth
☐ A piece of string, 6 inches longer than the radius of the cloth
☐ A stick of blackboard chalk
☐ A thumbtack
You should also find a large flat surface which will not be spoiled if a thumbtack is pushed into it, such as a wooden kitchen table.
Tie one end of the string around the blackboard chalk and measure the radius of the cloth from the chalk along the length of string. Mark this measurement by pushing the thumbtack through the string.
Lay the square of brown wrapping paper onto the flat surface

could upset the balance of your china when the table is set. Figures **4** and **5** show how to cut and join 48in widths to make a cloth with a diameter of 6ft 5in (77in).

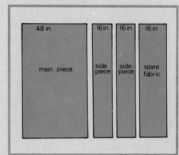

▲ **4.** *How to cut a 48in width*

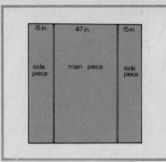

▲ **5.** *Joining the cut pieces*

Join the widths with a flat fell seam (see Home Sewing chapter 1, page 50).
You should now have a square of fabric with each side equal to the diameter of the cloth.

Cutting out
Fold the prepared square of fabric in half and then in half again, and pin the pattern onto the folded fabric as shown (figure **6**).

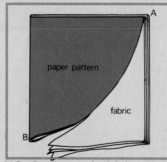

▲ **6.** *Cutting out the fabric*

Cut along the pattern edge. Unpin the pattern and unfold the fabric.

Making the hem
Snip little "V"'s into the edge at 1 inch intervals, $\frac{3}{8}$ inch deep (figure **7**).

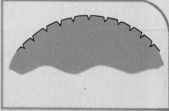

▲ **7.** *Snipping the hem edge*

Turn over the edge $\frac{1}{2}$ inch, pin and baste it down. The "V"'s will close up to allow the hem to curve (figure **8**).

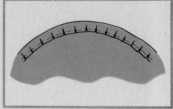

▲ **8.** *Turning over the $\frac{1}{2}$ inch hem*

Pin and baste the bias binding over the turned hem to cover the raw edge.
Stitch on the bias binding (figure **9**), finishing the ends by turning them under $\frac{1}{4}$ inch and overlapping them.

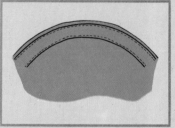

▲ **9.** *Stitching on bias binding*

Trimming
Machine stitch the trimming you have chosen around the edge of the tablecloth on the right side.

Good idea
For a round dining table in constant use, protect the tablecloth with a smaller cover made in the same fabric.
Cut a circle of plastic sheeting to the same diameter as that of the table top (this will protect the main cloth from spills), then make a smaller cloth with an overhang of about 6 inches, without trimming, to throw over the top.
This gives an all-over look to the table cover and only the smaller cover need be removed for quick and easy laundering.

and push the thumbtack into the top left-hand corner of the paper.
Hold the thumbtack firmly with one hand and draw an arc with the chalk from A, at the top right-hand corner of the paper, to B, at the bottom left-hand corner (figure **3**). Cut along the chalk line. The pattern is a quarter of the area of the cloth, and includes a $\frac{1}{2}$ inch hem allowance.

▼ **3.** *Making the paper pattern*

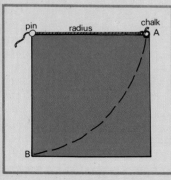

Making the cloth

You will need
☐ Fabric for the cloth
☐ Trimming of your own choice. The amount required is the length of the arc A to B multiplied by 4, plus 1 inch for overlapping. Some ideas for trimming are ball fringe, fringe, daisy chains or appliqué motifs
☐ Mercerized thread to match the fabric
☐ Matching bias binding (the same amount as for the trimming)
☐ Pins
☐ Basting thread

Preparing the fabric
If it is necessary to join the fabric, do so now. Join the pieces onto the sides of the main fabric piece; a seam across the middle of the cloth would be very noticeable and

Tunis and Tripoli braids

These attractive macramé patterns are fairly simple to work using the basic techniques of macramé. The result is, however, extremely effective—the pattern can be adapted to various yarns and the fabric produced can be made into lampshades, bags or belts. Experiment with wool, cotton, plastic raffia or even colored string.

Tunis braid

Set on double strands of 2 red, *6 white, 4 red. Repeat from * until required width is reached, finishing with 2 red.

Fix with one row of horizontal half hitches, making a 4-knot blackberry ball (See Macramé chapter 3, page 174) from the center 4 threads of each group of 8 red threads as you work.

1st row. On the first 4 red threads, work 2 rows diagonal half hitches as follows: Using 2nd thread as leader, work to left, then using 4th thread as leader, work across all 3 threads to left. Then work 3 rows of diagonal half hitches from left to right.

On the 12 white threads, knot pairs of threads in single knotted chains. (To make a single knotted chain take a pair of threads and, using alternate threads as leader, knot the other thread over it.) After 3 knots have been worked on each pair, unite all 12 threads in one large square knot. Continue in chains, working 3 knots on the 1st and 6th pairs of threads, 4 on the 2nd and 5th pairs, and 5 on the 3rd and 4th pairs. This gives a diamond shape.

On the next 8 red threads, using 1st thread as leader, work half hitches to the right across the next 3 threads. Then using 8th thread as leader, work to the left across the other 7 threads. (Once a leader has been taken across the work, it stays at the side in readiness for the next stage of the pattern, and the knotting is worked over an ever decreasing number of threads.) Continue working diagonal half hitches from left and right to make an inverted "V" taking the inner thread of the left-hand group and working it across to the right, then taking the inner thread of the right-hand group and working it across to the left. Continue in this way until each thread has been used as a leader. Repeat the pattern on following groups of red and white threads. At the end of the row, work 2 rows diagonal half hitches on the remaining red, using 1st thread as leader, working across all three threads to the right. Then make 3 rows of half hitches to the left.

2nd row. Work blocks of 4 rows of diagonal half hitches alternately left to right and right to left, using red threads as leaders.

3rd row. On the first 6 white threads, knot 3 pairs into single knotted chains, working 5 knots on the 1st pair, 4 on the 2nd pair and 3 on the 3rd. Unite all 6 threads into a square knot, then continue in chains, working the same number of knots as before on each pair.

On the next 8 red threads, work diagonal half hitches from left and right to make a "V" by taking 4th thread of left-hand group under 3rd thread and, using 3rd thread as leader, knot 4th thread onto it. Repeat this process with the 4th thread, using the 2nd thread

794

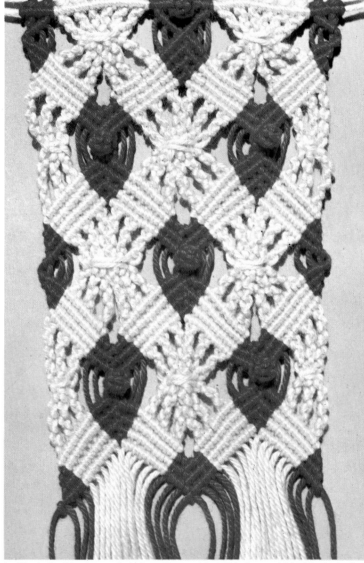

▲ *Tunis braid—knotted chains, diagonal half hitches and blackberry balls*

as leader and then the 1st. In this way, the thread works back on itself to the left. Do exactly the same on the right-hand group, taking the 1st thread behind and using 2nd, 3rd and 4th threads in turn as leader. Continue in this way by taking the inner thread of each group, alternating right and left, taking it behind the opposite group, and working it over each thread in turn as leader, until all the threads have been transferred.

Make a ball with the center 4 threads; then, starting with the inner threads, work diagonal half hitches from left and right to make an inverted "V" as in the 1st row.

On the 12 white threads knot pairs of threads into single knotted chains. Work 3 knots on the 1st and 6th pairs, 4 on the 2nd and 5th pairs and 5 on the 3rd and 4th pairs. Unite with a square knot, then continue chaining with the same number of knots. This results in a cluster of chains secured in the middle and forming a diamond shape.

Repeat pattern on following groups of red and white threads.

On the 6 white threads at the end of the row, reverse the number of knots on the chains from those at the beginning of the row, so that the longest chain is on the outer edge.

4th row. As 2nd row.

5th row. Take the 1st red thread behind and work over 2nd, 3rd and 4th as leaders in turn, as with the right-hand group in the

Tripoli cording—a combination of half hitches and square knots

4th as leaders in turn, as with the right-hand group in the diagonal half hitches forming a "V" in 3rd row. Continue until all threads have been worked. Then work 3 rows diagonal half hitches to the right. On the last group of red threads work 3 rows of diagonal half hitches to the right and then work the threads back on themselves, as with the left-hand group of the "V."

The rest of the row is the same as for 3rd row.

Continue working 3rd, 4th and 5th rows until required length is reached. With softer yarns a fringe can be worked following the lines of the pattern, but with stiffer yarns it is best to work half rows to even off the pattern and fix with one or two rows of horizontal half hitches.

Tripoli cording

Set on double strands as follows: 2 white, *4 green, 4 white, 4 green, 4 white, 4 green. Repeat from * until required width is reached, finishing with 2 white. Fix with one row of horizontal half hitches.

1st row. On first 4 white threads, work 4 rows diagonal half hitches as follows: Use the right-hand thread each time as leader in the first 2 rows and work from right to left. For the next 2 rows, work

from left to right, using the left-hand thread as leader.
*On the next 8 green threads work 4 rows of horizontal half hitches, using the same left-hand thread as leader throughout, zigzagging it back and forth. Work the 3rd thread over the 4th and the 6th over the 5th.
On the next 8 white threads work a square knot.
Repeat the green and white patterns along row from * until 4 white threads remain. Work these in the reverse order to the first 4.
2nd row. This consists of groups of 4 rows of diagonal half hitches using the green threads as leader. The first group is worked from right to left, the 2nd from left to right, and so on.
3rd row. As 1st, except on the left-hand group of green threads, where you should commence and finish by working the 2nd thread over the 1st, and on each complete group of green threads commence and finish by working the 3rd over the 4th and the 6th over the 5th. Then work as for 1st row. On the right-hand group of green threads, commence and finish by working the 3rd over the 4th. Repeat 2nd and 3rd rows until work is the required length. Complete with one row of horizontal half hitches.

To re-cover a lampshade
Prepare the frame in the usual way by painting and binding with tape. Choose a shape which is straight-sided and cut the doubled threads to at least four times the depth of the frame, plus the depth of fringe if you want one.
Set the threads directly onto the top of the frame so that the pattern will be completed between each set of struts. In addition, set one thread to each side of each strut. Fix all around with a row of horizontal half hitches.
Work a square knot braid over each strut to cover it. Then work the Tripoli cording to the depth of the shade, finishing with a row of horizontal half hitches. Finally knot the threads around the bottom of the frame and finish off either with a fringe or by darning in the ends. Lining a macramé shade is optional.

▼ *Tripoli cording makes a unique lampshade*

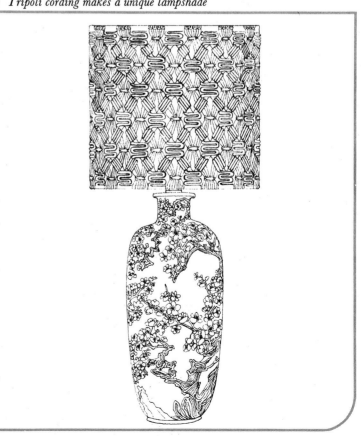

Tie-neck blouse conversion

The tie-neck blouse, shown here in a luxurious printed silk, is a soft and feminine variation of the Creative Hands basic blouse. In making it you will be taken several steps further in your dressmaking know-how. You will learn to apply couture finishes to a simple garment to turn it into something special, such as the finish on the sleeve openings which is especially suited to fine fabrics. This chapter, which includes layouts, goes to the fitting stage.

Suitable fabrics

You can use most of the fabrics mentioned for blouses in Dressmaking chapters 16, page 316, and 28, page 556, but for the gentle style of this tie-neck blouse the texture should be a little finer and the fabric quite soft. For instance, if you want to use a poplin, as for the basic blouse, make sure it is the fine type.

Yardages and notions

For yardages see layouts and note on tie collar on pages 798 and 799

☐ Interfacing, 36in width—the length of the blouse from the highest point on the shoulder to the hem plus 1½ inches for seams (see notes below)

☐ 8 buttons (you will need 2 more for link-buttoned cuffs)

☐ 1 small snap fastener

☐ Matching thread

A note on interfacing

The texture of the interfacing is dictated by the top fabric, i.e. soft fabric, soft interfacing.

To see if the texture of the interfacing is correct, make the following test. Place an edge of the interfacing into the folded edge of the top fabric—if the fabric rolls over the interfacing in a gentle, soft roll it is the right type to use. If, however, sharp points and a hard edge are formed, you have chosen the wrong texture of interfacing.

To help you in your choice, select from the following:

☐ For soft, natural fiber fabrics, choose a soft lawn or a finely textured pre-shrunk cotton, sold specifically for interfacing

☐ For soft fabrics in man-made fibers, pure silk organza is often the only choice, because an interfacing in a man-made fiber of the same type as the blouse fabric can result in edges which will not lie flat

The pattern pieces

For the tie-neck blouse you will need the following pattern pieces from the Creative Hands Pattern Pack given in Volume 22: from the basic blouse pattern sheet the Front and Back pattern pieces, numbers 1 and 2; from the accessory sheet the shirt sleeve, cuff and tie-collar pattern pieces, numbers 8, 12, 13 and 14.

The facing pattern

When making a garment in a soft fabric, it is advisable to avoid unnecessary seams—the finished garment will look smoother. So, when making the tie-neck blouse, the Front and front facing are cut out as one.

First make a facing pattern as shown in Dressmaking chapter 28, page 556, figure 3.

Then join the Front pattern piece to the facing pattern along the front edges by pinning them alongside each other over a strip of paper (figure 1 below). The line along the join becomes the fold line of the facing.

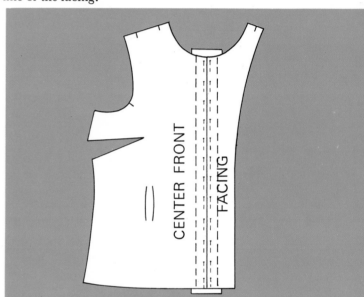

▲ 1. *Joining the Front and front facing patterns along the front edges*

Cutting out

Blouse fabric. Select the correct layout for your size from those given on the next 2 pages. Decide whether you want single or double cuffs (Dressmaking chapter 28) and a single or double width tie.

Pin the pattern pieces onto the fabric, mark out ¾ inch seam and hem allowances and cut out.

Mark all details on the fabric with tailor's tacks, using the methods shown so far.

After you have marked the blouse Front, unpin and remove the facing pattern, then mark along the front edge of the Front pattern piece for the fold line. Remove all pattern pieces.

Interfacing. First cut or tear off the selvages of the interfacing fabric.

Fold in half and pin the cuff and front facing patterns onto the double interfacing fabric. Cut a full cuff section or a half section only, depending on your choice of cuff.

Mark out ¾ inch seam allowances along the Front, hem, neck and shoulder edges of the facing and along the cuff edges.

You will not need seam allowances along the inner edge of the facing or along the fold edge of the single cuff.

Cut out and mark the pattern details on the interfacing.

Remove the pattern pieces.

Choose pure silk for the soft, gentle lines of the tie-neck blouse ►

Interfacing the Fronts for fitting

Pin and baste the interfacing to the wrong side of each blouse Front as shown (figure 2), allowing the seam allowance on the interfacing to go over the fold line onto the facing. Note that it is basted both along the Center Front and the fold line. Attach the interfacing to the blouse with small prick stitches (Dressmaking chapter 23, page 454). Work the prick stitches in the seam allowance of the interfacing, just outside the fold line, so that they will not show on the top of the garment when the facing is turned under.

Turn the facing to the inside and baste along the fold line ready for fitting.

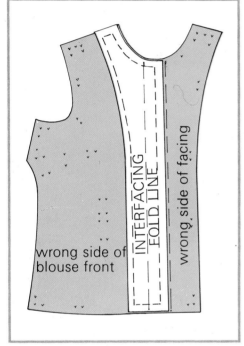

▲ 2. *The interfacing basted to the blouse Front*

Fitting the blouse

Carefully pin and baste the blouse darts and seams and baste in the sleeves ready for fitting.

Make any corrections necessary (Dressmaking chapter 16, page 316).

Fitting the collar

It is also necessary to fit the tie-neck collar before completing it. The balance marks on the ties are only an approximate indication of where the ties begin when the collar is attached to the neckline, and they will fall about 1 inch in from the Center Front at each side.

It is always best to determine how far a tie collar should be attached to the neckline by fitting. A given length may be right for one fabric but may leave an unsightly gap in another.

Two ways to finish the ties are given here. They can be folded in half lengthwise to achieve the effect in the picture, or made

798

double width and left unfolded with rolled hem edges. The latter is particularly attractive in transparent fabrics.

For both versions, first stitch the collar sections together along the Center Back line and press the seam open.

Folded collar version. To prepare this for fitting, fold the collar and ties in half lengthwise, right sides facing. Pin and baste the seams of the ties as far as the balance marks.

With the collar still inside out, pin and baste it to the blouse neckline, matching Center Backs, and with the balance marks falling on the Front neck edge 1 inch in from the Center Front at each side.

The wider collar. To prepare this for fitting, fold the collar lengthwise at the neck only. Pin and baste it to the blouse neckline, matching Center Backs, and with the balance marks falling on the Front neck edge 1 inch in from the Center Front at each side (figure 3).

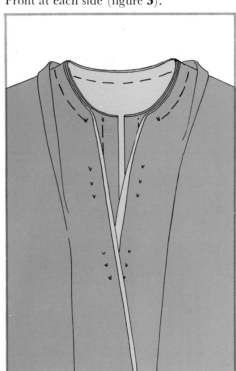

▲ 3. *Basting on the wider collar for fitting*

Both versions. Try on the blouse again and tie a bow to see how far you need the collar stitched to the blouse at the neck edge.

The bow should lie comfortably in the opening and not be pushed forward through lack of space. If it is, the size of the space must be increased equally on each side.

If, however, the space is too large, just reduce the distance equally on each side between the collar ends and the Center Front of the blouse.

Carefully mark the position of the collar ends on both the blouse and the collar.

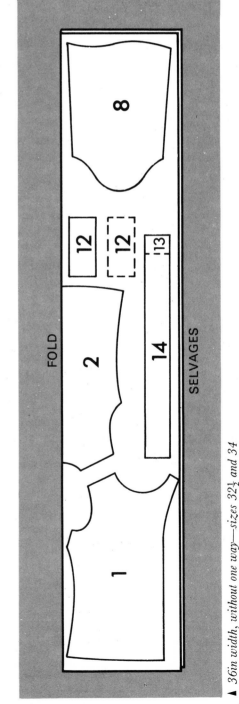

Yardages

36in width, without one way—sizes 32½ and 34, 2¾ yards; sizes 36 and 38, 3¾ yards; sizes 40 and 42, 3⅞ yards.

36in width, with one way—sizes 32½ and 34, 3 yards; size 36, 3⅜ yards; size 38, 3½ yards; sizes 40 and 42, 3¾ yards.

N.B. For transparent fabrics such as voile and chiffon, buy extra fabric and double the width of the tie collar to make a really full bow.

▲ *36in width, without one way—sizes 32½ and 34*

Key

Front=1   Cuff=12
Back=2   Right tie=13
Shirt sleeve=8   Left tie=14
Pattern in reverse = ⫽⫽⫽⫽⫽

▲ *36in width, without one way—sizes 36, 38, 40 and 42*

▼ *36in width, with one way—sizes 38, 40 and 42*

▲ *36in width, with one way—sizes 32½, 34 and 36*

Fashion Flair

Rose romance

This charming cross-stitch motif depicting a rose and snowball flower works equally well as a repeating border or separated into individual motifs. The dots on the chart represent cross-stitches worked in a contrast color. Alternatively, work them in a contrast texture of yarn.

1. Work the complete motif and top border to decorate a dainty evening bag. The lower border is formed by velvet ribbon.

2. Use a single rose motif to decorate a circular pincushion worked in cross-stitch.

3. Give a gypsy look to a blouse with long gathered sleeves and ruffle collar.

4. Short puff sleeves also lend themselves to the cross-stitch border. Add a single rose to a scarf as a finishing touch.

5. Accentuate inset pockets on an apron with the snowball flower motif.

Pattern Library

Flower dots

The pattern on printed fabrics can be used as a basis for decorative embroidery. Here, for example, large dots have been transformed into sprays of brightly colored flowers with simple stitches.

The petals are worked in lazy daisy stitch with a French knot at the center of each flower and at the base of each petal. The calyx are worked in satin stitch surrounded by a line of backstitch, and the stems are worked in outline stitch.

Flower dots like these would look particularly sweet on the yoke of a child's dress or the bib of a romper suit.

Knitting Know-how 41

Knitted lace stitches

Because of the lovely look they produce, lace stitches have always been among the most popular forms of knitting. Some of the most beautiful examples originated in the north of Scotland more than one hundred years ago. Many of these old stitches have charming names evoking their history and are recognized by knitters all over the world. Three of the most popular are given here, along with an ascot pattern which will help you practice candlelight stitch.

No matter how intricate these stitches may look, the patterns are really very simple to work. The principle is exactly the same as that explained in Knitting Know-how chapter 13, page 242, i.e., making an extra stitch by means of a loop and compensating for the extra stitch by working two stitches together somewhere in the pattern sequence. The decreased stitches may not necessarily be worked in the same row as the extra stitches, which means that on subsequent rows you will have more stitches than you started with. However, by the end of the number of rows needed to complete one whole pattern, you will have reverted to the correct number of stitches and will be ready to start the next repeat.

Traveling vine stitch

Cast on a number of stitches divisible by 8, plus 4.
1st row. Sl 1, K1, *ytf, K1 tbl, ytf, sl 1, K1, psso, K5, rep from * to last 2 sts, K2.
2nd row. Sl 1, P1, *P4, P2 tog tbl, P3, rep from * to last 2 sts, P1, K1.
3rd row. Sl 1, K1, *ytf, K1 tbl, ytf, K2, sl 1, K1, psso, K3, rep from * to last 2 sts, K2.
4th row. Sl 1, P1, * P2, P2 tog tbl, P5, rep from * to last 2 sts,

▼ *Traveling vine knitted lace stitch*

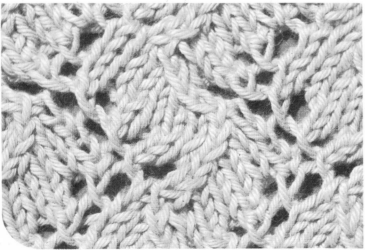

P1, K1.
5th row. Sl 1, K1, *K1 tbl, ytf, K4, sl 1, K1, psso, K1, ytf, rep from * to last 2 sts, K2.
6th row. Sl 1, P1, *P1, P2 tog tbl, P6, rep from * to last 2 sts, P1, K1.
7th row. Sl 1, K1, *K5, K2 tog, ytf, K1 tbl, ytf, rep from * to last 2 sts, K2.
8th row. Sl 1, P1, *P3, P2 tog, P4, rep from * to last 2 sts, P1, K1.
9th row. Sl 1, K1, *K3, K2 tog, K2, ytf, K1 tbl, ytf, rep from * to last 2 sts, K2.
10th row. Sl 1, P1, *P5, P2 tog, P2, rep from * to last 2 sts, P1, K1.
11th row. Sl 1, K1, *ytf, K1, K2 tog, K4, ytf, K1 tbl, rep from * to last 2 sts, K2.
12th row. Sl 1, P1, *P6, K2 tog, P1, rep from * to last 2 sts, P1, K1.
These 12 rows form pattern and are repeated throughout.

Fern stitch

Cast on a number of stitches divisible by 29, plus 2.
1st row. K1, *K1, sl 1, K2 tog, psso, K9, ytf, K1, yrn, P2, yon, K1, ytf, K9, sl 1, K2 tog, psso, rep from * to last st, K1.
2nd and every other row. P1, *P13, K2, P14, rep from * to last st, P1.
3rd row. K1, *K1, sl 1, K2 tog, psso, K8, ytf, K1, ytf, K1, P2, K1, ytf, K1, ytf, K8, sl 1, K2 tog, psso, rep from * to last st, K1.
5th row. K1, *K1, sl 1, K2 tog, psso, K7, ytf, K1, ytf, K2, P2, K2, ytf, K1, ytf, K7, sl 1, K2 tog, psso, rep from * to last st, K1.
7th row. K1, *K1, sl 1, K2 tog, psso, K6, ytf, K1, ytf, K3, P2, K3, ytf, K1, ytf, K6, sl 1, K2 tog, psso, rep from * to iast st, K1.
9th row. K1, *K1, sl 1, K2 tog, psso, K5, ytf, K1, ytf, K4, P2, K4, ytf, K1, ytf, K5, sl 1, K2 tog, psso, rep from * to last st, K1.
10th row. As 2nd.
These 10 rows form pattern and are repeated throughout. Note that when this pattern is completed it forms zigzag edges.

Candlelight stitch

Cast on a number of stitches divisible by 12, plus 1.
1st row. *K1, ytf, sl 1, K1, psso, K7, K2 tog, ytf, rep from * to last st, K1.
2nd and every other row. P to end.
3rd row. *K1, ytf, K1, sl 1, K1, psso, K5, K2 tog, K1, ytf, rep from * to last st, K1.
5th row. *K1, ytf, K2, sl 1, K1, psso, K3, K2 tog, K2, ytf, rep from * to last st, K1.
7th row. *K1, ytf, K3, sl 1, K1, psso, K1, K2 tog, K3, ytf, rep from * to last st, K1.
9th row. *K1, ytf, K4, sl 1, K2 tog, psso, K4, ytf, rep from * to last st, K1.
11th row. *K4, K2 tog, ytf, K1, ytf, sl 1, K1, psso, K3, rep from * to last st, K1.
13th row. *K3, K2 tog, K1, ytf, K1, ytf, K1, sl 1, K1, psso, K2, rep from * to last st, K1.
15th row. *K2, K2 tog, K2, ytf, K1, ytf, K2, sl 1, K1, psso, K1, rep from * to last st, K1.
17th row. *K1, K2 tog, K3, ytf, K1, ytf, K3, sl 1, K1, psso, rep from * to last st, K1.
19th row. K2 tog, *K4, ytf, K1, ytf, K4, sl 1, K2 tog, psso, rep from * ending last rep sl 1, K1, psso.
20th row. As 2nd.
These 20 rows form pattern and are repeated throughout.

Fern stitch with a leafy look

▼*Candlelight stitch, used for the ascot*

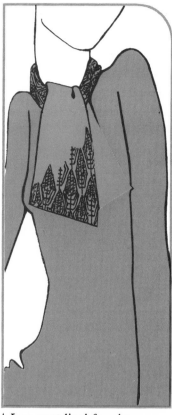

▲ *Lacy ascot lined for crispness*

Ascot in lacy candlelight stitch

Size
8in wide by 30in long

Gauge
$8\frac{1}{2}$ sts and $10\frac{1}{2}$ rows to 1in over stockinette stitch worked on No.2 needles.

Materials
3-ply baby yarn
7 1oz skeins
One pair No.2 needles
(or Canadian No.11)
$\frac{1}{4}$yd of 36in wide lining material

Ascot
Using No.2 needles, cast on 73 sts.
Rep 20 patt rows given for candlelight stitch 16 times in all. Bind off.

Finishing
Press lightly on WS under a damp cloth with a warm iron. Cut lining to fit ascot. With WS of ascot facing WS of lining, seam one short and 2 long ends. Turn to RS and sl st rem short end.

Authentic Aran cardigan

One charm of authentic Aran designs is that they suit both men and women.

Sizes
Directions are for 36in bust or chest.
The figures in brackets [] refer to the 38, 40, 42 and 44in sizes respectively.
Length down center back, 24[24½:25:25½:26]in, adjustable.
Sleeve seam, 17[17½:18:18½: 19]in, adjustable.

Gauge
5 sts and 7 rows to 1in over double seed stitch worked on No.6 needles.

Materials
Bernat Blarney-Spun 10[11:12:12:13] 2oz balls
One pair No.3 needles (or Canadian No.10)
One pair No.6 needles (or Canadian No.7)
One cable needle
Two stitch holders
Five buttons

Back

Using No.3 needles, cast on 94[98:102:106:110] sts.
1st row *K1 tbl, P1, rep from * to end.
Rep 1st row 7 times more.
Next row K to end, inc 16 sts evenly across row. 110[114:118:122:126] sts.
Change to No.6 needles.
1st row (wrong side) (K1, P1) 3[4:5:6:7] times, *K2, P6, K7, P4, K6, P6, K2*, P32 sts, rep from * to * once, (K1, P1) 3[4:5:6:7] times.
2nd row (K1, P1) 3[4:5:6:7] times, *P2, sl next 2 sts onto cable needle and hold at back of work, K2, K2 from cable needle—called C4B—K2, P6, K2, sl next 2 sts onto cable needle and hold at front of work, P1, K2 from cable needle—called K2F—P6, C4B, K2, P2*, (C4B, sl next 2 sts onto cable needle and hold at front of work, K2, K2 from cable needle—called C4F) 4 times, rep from * to * once, (K1, P1) 3[4:5:6:7] times.
3rd row (P1, K1) 3[4:5:6:7] times, *K2, P6, K6, P2, K1, P2, K6, P6, K2*, P32 sts, rep from * to * once, (P1, K1) 3[4:5:6:7] times.
4th row (P1, K1) 3[4:5:6:7] times, *P2, K6, P5, sl next st onto cable needle and hold at back of work, K2, P1 from cable needle—called P1B—K1, K2F, P5, K6, P2*, K32 sts, rep from * to * once, (P1, K1) 3[4:5:6:7] times.
5th row (K1, P1) 3[4:5:6:7] times, *K2, P6, K5, P2, K1, P1, K1, P2, K5, P6, K2*, P32 sts, rep from * to * once, (K1, P1) 3[4:5:6:7] times.
6th row (K1, P1) 3[4:5:6:7] times, *P2, K2, C4F, P4, P1B, K1, P1, K1, K2F, P4, K2, C4F, P2*, (C4F, C4B) 4 times, rep from * to * once, (K1, P1) 3[4:5:6:7] times.
7th row (P1, K1) 3[4:5:6:7] times, *K2, P6, K4, P2, (K1, P1) twice, K1, P2, K4, P6, K2*, P32 sts, rep from * to * once, (P1, K1) 3[4:5:6:7] times.
8th row (P1, K1) 3[4:5:6:7] times, *P2, K6, P3, P1B, (K1, P1) twice, K1, K2F, P3, K6, P2*, K32 sts, rep from

* to * once, (P1, K1) 3[4:5:6:7] times.
9th row (K1, P1) 3[4:5:6:7] times, *K2, P6, K3, P2, (K1, P1) 3 times, K1, P2, K3, P6, K2*, P32 sts, rep from * to * once, (K1, P1) 3[4:5:6:7] times.
10th row (K1, P1) 3[4:5:6:7] times, *P2, C4B, K2, P2, P1B, (K1, P1) 3 times, K1, K2F, P2, C4B, K2, P2*, (C4B, C4F) 4 times, rep from * to * once, (K1, P1) 3[4:5:6:7] times.
11th row (P1, K1) 3[4:5:6:7] times, *K2, P6, K2, P2, (K1, P1) 4 times, K1, P2, K2, P6, K2*, P32 sts, rep from * to * once, (P1, K1) 3[4:5:6:7] times.
12th row (P1, K1) 3[4:5:6:7] times, *P2, K6, P1, P1B, (K1, P1) 4 times, K1, K2F, P1, K6, P2*, K32 sts, rep from * to * once, (P1, K1) 3[4:5:6:7] times.
13th row (K1, P1) 3[4:5:6:7] times, *K2, P6, K1, P2, (K1, P1) 5 times, K1, P2, K1, P6, K2*, P32 sts, rep from * to * once, (K1, P1) 3[4:5:6:7] times.
14th row (K1, P1) 3[4:5:6:7] times, *P2, K2, C4F, P1, K2F, (P1, K1) 4 times, P1, P1B, P1, K2, C4F, P2*, (C4F, C4B) 4 times, rep from * to * once, (K1, P1) 3[4:5:6:7] times.
15th row (P1, K1) 3[4:5:6:7] times, *K2, P6, K2, P2, (K1, P1) 4 times, K1, P2, K2, P6, K2*, P32 sts, rep from * to * once, (P1, K1) 3[4:5:6:7] times.
16th row (P1, K1) 3[4:5:6:7] times, *P2, K6, P2, K2F, (P1, K1) 3 times, P1, P1B, P2, K6, P2*, K32 sts, rep from * to * once, (P1, K1) 3[4:5:6:7] times.
17th row As 9th.
18th row (K1, P1) 3[4:5:6:7] times, *P2, C4B, K2, P3, K2F, (P1, K1) twice, P1, P1B, P3, C4B, K2, P2*, (C4B, C4F) 4 times, rep from * to * once, (K1, P1) 3[4:5:6:7] times.
19th row As 7th.
20th row (P1, K1) 3[4:5:6:7] times, *P2, K6, P4, K2F, P1, K1, P1, P1B, P4, K6, P2*, K32 sts, rep from * to * once,

(P1, K1) 3[4:5:6:7] times.
21st row As 5th.
22nd row (K1, P1) 3[4:5:6:7] times, *P2, K2, C4F, P5, K2F, P1, P1B, P5, K2, C4F, P2*, (C4F, C4B) 4 times, rep from * to * once, (K1, P1) 3[4:5:6:7] times.
23rd row As 3rd.
24th row (P1, K1) 3[4:5:6:7] times, *P2, K6, P6, sl next 3 sts onto cable needle and hold at front of work, K2, K2, P1 from cable needle, P6, K6, P2*, K32 sts, rep from * to * once, (P1, K1) 3[4:5:6:7] times.
These 24 rows form patt and are rep throughout back.
Continue in patt until work measures 15[15½:16:16½:17] in or required length to underarm, ending with a WS row.

Shape armholes
Bind off 8 sts at beg of next 2 rows.
1st raglan row K1, sl 1, K1, psso, patt to last 3 sts, K2 tog, K1.
2nd raglan row K1, P1, patt to last 2 sts, P1, K1.
Rep these 2 rows until 32 [34:36:38:40] sts rem.
Bind off.

Left front

Using No.3 needles, cast on 29 sts.
Work 24 rows K1, P1 rib for pocket lining.
Slip sts on holder.
Using No.3 needles, cast on 48[50:52:54:56] sts.
Work 8 rows twisted rib as given for back.
Next row K to end, inc 8 sts evenly across row. 56[58:60:62:64] sts.
Change to No.6 needles.
Commence patt.
1st row (wrong side) K1, P16, K2, P6, K7, P4, K6, P6, K2, (K1, P1) 3[4:5:6:7] times.
2nd row (K1, P1) 3[4:5:6:7] times, P2, C4B, K2, P6, K2, K2F, P6, C4B, K2, P2, (C4B, C4F) twice, K1.
Continue in patt as given until 24 rows have been worked, K front edge st on every row.

804

Next row K1, P16, K2, sl next 29 sts onto stitch holder, work in patt across 29 pocket lining sts, K2, (K1, P1) 3[4:5:6:7] times.
Continue until work measures same as back to armhole, ending at armhole edge.

Shape armhole and neck
Next row Bind off 8 sts, patt to last 2 sts, dec one. Work 1 row.

▲ *Stitch details of Aran patterns*

Next row K1, Sl 1, K1, psso, patt to end.
Next row Dec one, patt to last 3 sts, P1, K1.
Continue in this way, dec one st at armhole edge on every other row and one st at neck edge on every 3rd row 16[17:18:19:20] times in all, until all sts are worked off. Pull yarn through last st. Fasten off.

Right front

Work as given for left front, reading patt row in reverse and reversing all shapings.

Sleeves

Using No.3 needles, cast on 46[48:50:52:54] sts.
Work 3in twisted rib as given for back.
Next row K to end, inc 14 sts evenly across row. 60[62:64:66:68] sts.
Change to No.6 needles.
1st row K1[K2:P1, K2:K1, P1, K2:P1, K1, P1, K2], P6, K2, P16, K2, P6, K2, P16, K2, P6, K1[K2:K2, P1: K2, P1, K1:K2, P1, K1,

P1].
2nd row P1[P2:K1, P2: P1, K1, P2:K1, P1, K1, P2], C4B, K2, P2, (C4B, C4F) twice, P2, C4B, K2, P2, (C4B, C4F) twice, P2, C4B, K2, P1[P2:P2, K1:P2, K1, P1:P2, K1, P1, K1].
Continue in patt as given, working 2 honeycomb panels and 3 plaited cables and inc one st at each end of next and every 6th row until there are 80[84:88:92:96] sts. Work inc in double seed st.
Continue without shaping until sleeve measures 17 [17½:18:18½:19]in or desired length, ending with a WS row.

Shape cap
Bind off 8 sts at beg of next 2 rows.
Work 1st and 2nd raglan rows as given for back until 2[4:6:8:10]sts rem.
Bind off.

Buttonhole band

Using No.3 needles, cast on 10 sts. Work in twisted rib as given for back.
Work 3 rows.
Next row Rib 4.sts, bind off 2 sts, rib 4 sts.
Next row Rib 4 sts, cast on 2 sts, rib 4 sts.
Continue in rib working 4 more buttonholes in this way at 3[3¼:3½:3¾:4]in intervals, until band measures 56[58: 60:62:64]in when slightly stretched.
Bind off.

Finishing

Using No.3 needles and with RS pocket top facing, work 7 rows twisted rib as given for back. Bind off. Complete other pocket top in same way. Sew in sleeves. Join side and sleeve seams. Sew around pocket linings and sides of pocket tops. Sew on buttonhole band, with buttonholes on left front for a man's garment and right front for a woman's. Sew on buttons to correspond to buttonholes. Press lightly under a damp cloth with a warm iron.

Crocheted curtain

Crocheted curtains can revive the charm of yesterday's furnishings and this one is designed using a motif which suits both traditional and modern decors. The same pattern can also be used to make a bedspread.

Measurements
One motif measures approx. 12sq in.

Gauge
8dc and 4 rows to 1in worked on No.B crochet hook.

Materials
Curtain One motif takes approximately 2¼ balls of Coats & Clark's O.N.T. Pearl Cotton
Edging One ball works approximately 17in of edging
One No.B (2.00 mm) crochet hook

Note
All rounds begin with 2dc in loop. This is worked as follows: Ch3, 1dc into loop worked last in previous round. This applies only to the first 2dc of each round. All rounds are joined with a ss.

Motif

Using No.B crochet hook, ch6. Join with a ss into first ch to form circle.
1st round Ch3, 2dc into circle, ch3, *3dc into circle, ch3, rep from * twice. Join with a ss.
2nd round *2dc into loop, 1dc into each of next 3dc, into

ch3 loop work 2dc, ch3, rep from * 3 times. Join with a ss.
3rd round *2dc into loop, 1dc into each of next 3dc, into next dc work 4dc, take hook out of last st and insert it into first of 4dc, draw loop from fourth dc through first to form cluster—called 1cl— 1dc into each of next 3dc, 2dc into ch3 loop, ch3, rep from * 3 times. Join with a ss.
4th round *2dc into loop, 1dc into each of next 3dc, (1cl into next dc, 1dc into each of next 3dc) twice, 2dc into corner ch3 loop, ch3, rep from * 3 times. Join with a ss.
5th round *2dc into loop, 3dc, (1cl, 3dc) 3 times, 2dc into corner ch3 loop, ch3, rep from * 3 times.
6th round *2dc into loop, 3dc, (1cl, 3dc) 4 times, 2dc into corner ch3 loop, ch3, rep from * 3 times.
7th round *2dc into loop, 2dc, ch8, 5dc, (1cl, 3dc) 3 times, 2dc, ch8, 2dc, 2dc into corner ch3 loop, ch3, rep from * 3 times.
8th round *2dc into loop, 2dc, ch4, 1sc into ch8 loop, ch4, skip 2dc, 5dc, (1cl, 3dc) twice, 2dc, ch4, 1sc into ch8 loop, ch4, skip 2dc, 2dc, 2dc into corner ch3 loop, ch3, rep from * 3 times.
9th round *2dc into loop, 2dc, ch4, 1sc into loop, 1sc into sc, 1sc into loop, ch4, skip 2dc, 5dc, 1cl, 5dc, ch4, 1sc into loop, 1sc into sc, 1sc into loop, ch4, skip 2dc, 2dc, 2dc into corner ch3 loop, ch3, rep from * 3 times.
10th round *2dc into loop, 2dc, ch4, 1sc into loop, 3sc, 1sc into loop, ch4, skip 2dc, 7dc, ch4, 1sc into loop, 3sc,

1sc into loop, ch4, skip 2dc, 2dc, 2dc into corner ch3 loop, ch3, rep from * 3 times.
11th round *2dc into loop, 2dc, ch4, 1sc into loop, 5sc, 1sc into loop, ch4, skip 2dc, 3dc, ch4, 1sc into loop, 5sc, 1sc into loop, ch4, skip 2dc, 2dc, 2dc into corner ch3 loop, ch3, rep from * 3 times.
12th round *2dc into loop, 4dc, 2dc into next loop, ch4, skip 1sc, 5sc, ch4, 2dc into next loop, 3dc, 2dc into next loop, ch4, skip 1sc, 5sc, ch4, 2dc into next loop, 4dc, 2dc into corner ch3 loop, ch3, rep from * 3 times.
13th round *2dc into loop, 8dc, 2dc into next loop, ch4, skip 1sc, 3sc, ch4, 2dc in next loop, 7dc, 2dc into next loop, ch4, skip 1sc, 3sc, ch4, 2dc into next loop, 8dc, 2dc into corner ch3 loop, ch3, rep from * 3 times.
14th round *2dc into loop, 12dc, 2dc into next loop, ch4, skip 1sc, 1sc, ch4, 2dc into next loop, 11dc, 2dc into next loop, ch4, skip 1sc, 1sc, ch4, 2dc into next loop, 12dc, 2dc into corner ch3 loop, ch3, rep from * 3 times.
15th round *2dc into loop, 16dc, 2dc into loop, 2dc into next loop, 15dc, 2dc into loop, 2dc into next loop, 16dc, 2dc into corner ch3 loop, ch3, rep from * 3 times.
16th round *2dc into loop, (1dc into next dc, ch1, skip 1dc) 29 times, 1dc into last dc, 2dc into corner ch3 loop, ch3, rep from * 3 times.
17th round *2dc into loop, 3dc, (1dc into dc, 1dc into ch) 29 times, 3dc, 2dc into corner ch3 loop, ch3, rep from * 3 times.
18th round *2dc into loop, 3dc, (1cl, 3dc) 16 times, 2dc into corner ch3 loop, ch3, rep from * 3 times.
19th round *2dc into loop, 3dc, (1cl, 3dc) 17 times, 2dc into corner ch3 loop, ch3, rep from * 3 times.
20th round *2dc into loop, 1dc into each st to next corner, 2dc into corner ch3 loop, ch3, rep from * 3 times.
21st round *2dc into loop, (1dc into next dc, ch1, skip 1dc) 39 times, 1dc into last dc,

1sc into loop, ch4, skip 2dc, 2dc, 2dc into corner ch3 loop, ch3, rep from * 3 times.
22nd round *2dc into loop, 2dc, (1dc into dc, 1dc into ch) 39 times, 3dc, 2dc into corner ch3 loop, ch3, rep from * 3 times.
23rd round *2dc into loop, 3dc, (1cl, 3dc) 6 times, 36dc, (1cl, 3dc) 6 times, 2dc into corner ch3 loop, ch3, rep from * 3 times.
24th round *2dc into loop, 3dc, 1cl, (ch1, skip 1dc, 1dc into next dc) 9 times, ch1, skip 1dc, 1cl, 21dc, 1cl, 21dc, 1cl, (ch1, skip 1dc, 1dc into next dc) 9 times, ch1, skip 1dc, 1cl, 3dc, 2dc into corner ch3 loop, ch3, rep from * 3 times.
25th round *2dc into loop, 3dc, 1cl, (ch1, skip 1ch, 1dc) 9 times, ch1, 1cl into next dc, 21dc, 1cl, 3dc, 1cl, 21dc, 1cl, (ch1, skip 1dc, 1dc) 9 times, ch1, 1cl, 3dc, 2dc into corner ch3 loop, ch3, rep from * 3 times.
26th round *2dc into loop, 3dc, 1cl, (ch1, skip 1st, 1dc) 9 times, ch1, skip 1st, 1cl, 21dc, 1cl, (ch1, skip 1st, 1dc) 3 times, ch1, skip 1st, 1cl, 21dc, 1cl, (ch1, skip 1st, 1dc) 9 times, ch1, skip 1st, 1cl, 3dc, 2dc into corner ch3 loop, ch3, rep from * 3 times.
27th round *2dc into loop, 3dc, 1cl, (ch1, skip 1st, 1dc) 9 times, ch1, skip 1st, 1cl, 21dc, 1cl, (ch1, skip 1st, 1dc) 5 times, ch1, skip 1st, 1cl, 21dc, 1cl, (ch1, skip 1st, 1dc) 9 times, ch1, skip 1st, 1cl, 3dc, 2dc into corner ch3 loop, ch3, rep from * 3 times.
Fasten off. Darn in all ends.

Edging

Using No.B crochet hook, ch40.

1st row Insert hook into 5th ch from hook, 1sc, ch2, skip 2ch, *1dc into each of next 2ch, 5dc into next ch, take hook out of last dc and insert into first of 5dc, draw through loop of 5th dc to form cluster—called large cl—1dc into each of next 2ch, ch2, skip 2ch, 1sc into next ch, ch2, skip 2ch, rep from * once, 1dc into each of next 15ch. Turn.

2nd row Ch2, 13dc between dc, ch4, 1sc into next ch loop, *ch4, 1sc into next ch loop, rep from * 3 times. Turn.

3rd row Ch4, 1sc into ch loop, ch2, *work 2dc, 1 large cl, 2dc into next ch loop, ch2, 1sc into next ch loop, ch2, rep from * once, skip 2dc, 12dc between dc. Turn.

4th row Ch2, 10dc between dc, *ch4, 1sc into next ch loop, rep from * 4 times. Turn.

5th row Ch4, 1sc into loop, ch2, *work 2dc, 1 large cl, 2dc into next ch loop, ch2, 1sc into next loop, ch2, rep from * once, skip 2dc, 9dc between dc. Turn.

6th row Ch2, 7dc between dc, *ch4, 1sc into next ch loop, rep from * 4 times. Turn.

7th row Ch4, 1sc into next loop, ch2, *work 2dc, 1 large cl, 2dc into next loop, ch2, 1sc into next loop, ch2, rep from * once, 6dc between dc. Turn.

8th row Ch2, 4dc between dc, *ch4, 1sc into next loop, rep from * 4 times. Turn.

9th row Ch7, 1sc into next loop, ch2, *work 2dc, 1 large cl, 2dc into next loop, ch2, 1sc into next loop, ch2, rep from * once, 3dc between dc. Turn.

10th row Ch2, 2dc between dc, 2dc into next loop, *ch4, 1sc into next loop, rep from * 4 times. Turn.

11th row Ch7, insert hook in 5th ch, 1sc, ch2, * work 2dc, 1 large cl, 2dc into next loop, ch2, 1sc into next loop, ch2, rep from * once, 2dc into next loop, 4dc between dc. Turn.

12th row Ch2, 5dc between dc, 2dc into loop, *ch4, 1sc into next loop, rep from * 4 times. Turn.

13th row Ch7, 1sc into 5th of 7ch, ch2, *work 2dc, 1 large cl, 2dc into next loop, ch2, 1sc into next loop, ch2, rep from * once, 2dc into loop, 7dc between dc. Turn.

14th row Ch2, 8dc between dc, 2dc into next loop, *ch4, 1sc into next loop, rep from * 4 times. Turn.

15th row Ch7, 1sc into 5th of 7ch, ch2, *work 2dc, 1 large cl, 2dc into next loop, ch2,

1sc into next loop, ch2, rep from * once, 2dc into next loop, 10dc between dc. Turn.

16th row Ch2, 11dc between dc, 2dc into next loop, *ch4, 1sc into next loop, rep from * 4 times. Turn.

Rep from 1st to 16th rows

for required length working 1st row as follows:
Ch7, 1sc into 5th of 7ch, ch2, *2dc, 1 large cl, 2dc into next loop, ch2, 1sc into next loop, ch2, rep from * once, 2dc into next loop, 13dc between dc. Turn.

Finishing

Press each motif and edging under a damp cloth.
Curtain shown here consists of 7 rows with 4 motifs in each row. Sew or crochet motifs tog, sew on edging.

Free stitch varieties

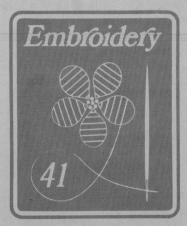

A great variety of stitches and techniques are used to obtain effects in free-motion embroidery, and this chapter gives detailed instructions on how to set up the sewing machine to achieve these effects.

The dress and bolero outfit featured in this chapter is an original design, and the pattern is unfortunately not available. There are, however, several commercial paper patterns on the market which could easily be adapted to make a similar dress or bolero. A tracing pattern is provided on pages 810 and 811 as a guide to the embroidery on the bolero.

What could be a more charming going-away outfit than this for a spring or summer wedding? It is a perfect ensemble for any occasion.

Once the basic running and zigzag stitches are mastered, more advanced free-motion embroidery stitches can be tried. These are made by altering machine tension, using thicker or metallic threads on the bobbin, or by catching threads too thick to use on the machine to the background fabric.

Whip Stitch

Tightly stretch the fabric to be embroidered into a hoop. Remove the presser foot, lower the feed teeth, and set the machine for running stitch. Loosen the bobbin tension from normal and tighten the top tension. This brings the bottom thread to the top of the work, making a beady

corded stitch much thicker than the basic running stitch. To produce a good neat stitch, move the hoop smoothly and slowly so that the little loops are close to one another. The top thread should not be seen. If the tensions are altered even more (by loosening the bobbin and tightening the top tension still further), a very exaggerated, spiky stitch results because the top thread is so tight. This stitch is best worked into circular shapes because it can then lie flat on the background fabric. A slightly thicker thread used on the bobbin gives an even more pronounced effect.

The choice of thread must be determined by the weave of the background fabric because thick threads will not pull easily through a tightly woven cloth.

When altering tensions, either on top of the machine or in the bobbin, make the alteration gradually, trying out the effect between each change.

Working in thicker threads

Begin by setting the machine for running stitch.

Thicker threads such as pearl cotton No.5 and 8, 6-strand floss, thin yarn and metallic threads are wound onto the bobbin by hand as described in Embroidery chapter 26, p. 508. Machine embroidery thread or mercerized sewing thread, is used on top of the machine. The work is stitched face downward because the interesting thread is in the bobbin. Bobbin tension should be loose and top tension either normal or slightly tight for working

A striking example of the use of machine embroidery for fashion

with these types of thread. If the speed of the needle is kept steady and the fabric moved smoothly, a cording effect will result. For really thick threads, keep the bobbin tension quite loose or it will pull too much on the background cloth.

Toweling stitch

With pearl cotton, 6-strand floss or thin wool on the bobbin, a more loopy effect can be obtained by loosening the bobbin tension even more and tightening the top tension. By pushing the hoop slowly under the needle, the loops have time to build up.

For a greater looped effect using a thick yarn, such as sports yarn, completely remove

the tension screw on the bobbin case. The free or darning foot is used so that larger areas of fabric can be covered at any one time without using a hoop. Always remember to lower the presser foot lever whether the foot is on the machine or not, as this engages the top tension.

Metal threads

Only metal threads which are specifically made for machine embroidery will stitch through fabric. Other kinds break and should be wound onto the bobbin by hand and worked from the wrong side.

Providing the fabric is not too tightly woven, Lurex thread can be used for whip stitch. In this case, the thread on

Drawn threads worked with zigzag

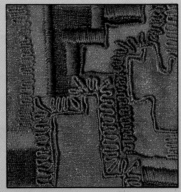

Embroidery on a printed organza

Whip stitch decorated with sequins

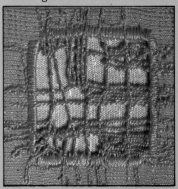

Toweling stitch with thick wool

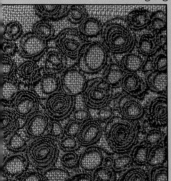

Whip stitch worked in fine circles

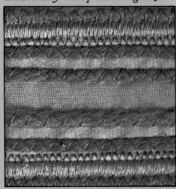

Thicker threads couched with zigzag

Flower design in fine whip stitch

Whip stitch decorated square hole

Satin stitch with metal thread

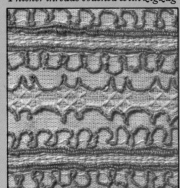

Design worked around fabric weave

Whip stitch in gold with beads

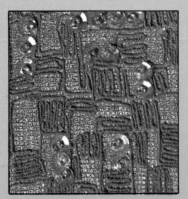

Toweling stitch with pearl cotton

top must not show. When using metal threads, work very smoothly and at a slightly slower speed than with other kinds of threads. This is because a sudden jerk will snap the metal thread.

If you are working zigzag or straight stitch, the tension of the metal thread needs to be slightly looser than the top thread. The top thread remains on the wrong side of the work, the metal thread is smooth and the work completely metallic on the right side. If the metal thread is of a type which can be used on top of the machine, a larger needle should be used. Metallic threads look especially rich and decorative when used in zigzag stitch.

Fabric with unusual weaves
Zigzag stitch can be used most successfully on soft and open-weave fabrics. A pulled fabric effect results on open-weave fabrics, such as linen scrim, open home furnishing nets etc., by working with machine embroidery thread with both tensions slightly tighter than normal. The zigzag stitch pulls the open-weave threads together and small motifs can be worked leaving large areas of the background fabric unworked. Alternatively, cover the fabric completely with hundreds of zigzag stitches touching each other so that the finished result is rich and textured. The best results with this technique are obtained with the fabric held

in a hoop.

For drawn threadwork and machine embroidery, choose loose-weave fabrics such as scrim, burlap or linen, and pull out the warp or weft threads (or both) using different widths of zigzag stitches. The effect is particularly interesting where the fabric is made of two colors and the threads pulled out in either direction so that one color remains.

Embroidering holes
Lacy effects are worked by using zigzag stitches around a shape in the design and then cutting the inside fabric away, leaving a hole. For a spider's web effect, for example, work

running stitch across the hole and then strengthen the stitches with a small zigzag stitch. To achieve this, the fabric must be in a hoop and the tension of top and bottom threads exactly equal so that they twist around each other when worked across the space.

Very thick textured threads
Any thread which is too thick to be wound onto the bobbin, or too textured to pull through, can be caught to the fabric with a running or zigzag stitch. This method of couching by machine using the ordinary or free foot can be worked using knitting yarn, weaving yarn, string, raffia, ribbons, tapes or braids.

Free fashion embroidery

To make a bolero like the one illustrated, which was made in a washable synthetic fabric, first choose a commercial paper pattern and mark the outline of the garment onto the fabric. Some of the stitches described in this chapter have been incorporated into the bolero. The embroidery design is not repetitive, but we give guide lines to trace for one front, plus a large flower motif, which the more experienced embroiderer could adapt for the back of the garment. Use a hoop and either follow the guide accurately or improvise with your own ideas.

Do not cut out the pattern pieces until the embroidered design has been worked. Once the embroidery is finished, make the bolero according to the pattern instructions.

Trace the outline of the design on these pages and use as a guide for free-motion embroidery

Covering a stool in needlepoint

If a favorite footstool shows signs of wear on the top fabric, it is a relatively simple matter to work a new top in needlepoint to re-cover it. The stitches shown in this chapter suggest stripes which make a colorful topping for stools.

Needlepoint is particularly suitable for footstool tops because it is so hard-wearing. For the best results the important thing to bear in mind is always to use the best quality yarns and canvas. Also, special care must be taken when planning the design as this must look equally good from every angle. The stitches shown on these pages suggest stripes, which can be most attractive when worked in carefully selected colors.

Materials you will need
- ☐ Canvas (To assess the amount required, measure across the width of the stool top, plus the drop on both sides. Measure in the same way for the length and add 6 inches to each measurement to allow for blocking.)
- ☐ Muslin of a similar amount
- ☐ Soft lead pencil
- ☐ Dressmakers' pins
- ☐ Tapestry yarn or crewel yarn in the amounts specified for the design chosen
- ☐ Tapestry needle No.18
- ☐ Fine ½in upholstery tacks for corners
- ☐ Brass-headed upholstery tacks (sufficient to go around the stool placed closely together)

Before you begin
Remove the old covering and make sure that the existing padding is firm and even. If not, the top should be re-upholstered.

Making a pattern
Working out the shape of the pattern is first done with muslin, just like a muslin in dressmaking. The muslin must be made bigger than the seat area and the drop. Using a soft pencil, mark a vertical and horizontal line from side to side across the center of the muslin, using the thread of the weave as a guide.

Draw similar center lines on the stool. Place the muslin on the stool, matching the lines. Pin the muslin to the stool top, starting at the center of the crossed lines and working out simultaneously to all four sides, placing the pins at 3 inch intervals. Continue these lines of pins down the depth of the drop. Pin the corners to make miters.

With a soft pencil, mark the area of the top of the stool, the edge of the frame and both sides of each mitered corner.

Take the muslin off the stool and measure the length and width of the muslin to make sure that it corresponds exactly to the measurements of the stool. If it does not, the muslin has been pulled out of shape.

Working on a firm surface, pin the muslin onto brown paper, making sure that the weave of the muslin is straight. The pattern on the muslin may be slightly irregular, but make the brown paper pattern absolutely symmetrical. Mark the vertical

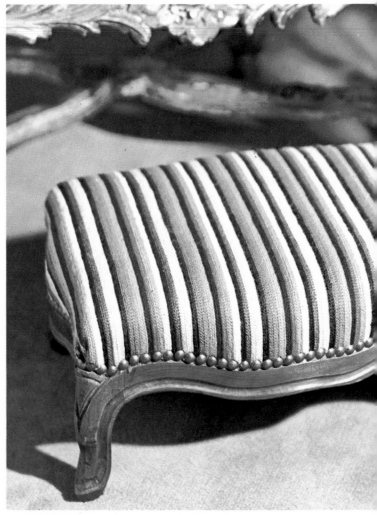

▲ An example of a footstool top worked in stripes of chain stitch

and horizontal lines on the canvas to match up with those on the paper pattern. Pin the pattern to the canvas and mark with a felt pen around the edge. This gives the area of the canvas to be worked. Cut the canvas to a square leaving at least a 3 inch margin all around for blocking.

Covering the stool
When you have completed stitching the design on the canvas for the stool cover, block and trim the work as described in Needlepoint chapter 5, page 112, leaving the unworked areas of canvas in the corners for mitering. Turn the seam allowances to the back of the work and and secure with basting thread.

Fit the cover over the stool, matching the center lines, and hammer in a brass-headed tack at each of the four points where these lines end. Pad

the head of the hammer with cloth to prevent damage to the tacks.

Smooth the canvas out from two of these center points on adjacent sides, working toward the corner and tacking with brass-headed tacks as you go. Fix the point of the canvas corner to the stool using an upholstery tack and then ease the edges of the worked canvas together to meet at the corner edge (see diagram).

Work the remaining corners in the same way, working the diagonally opposite corner next.

Working the canvas
Chain stitch method 1. This is a very quick method worked with a fine crochet hook, skipping two holes of the canvas with each stitch. For a shorter stitch, skip one hole each time, for a longer one, skip more. Do not make the stitches too long or the work will wear

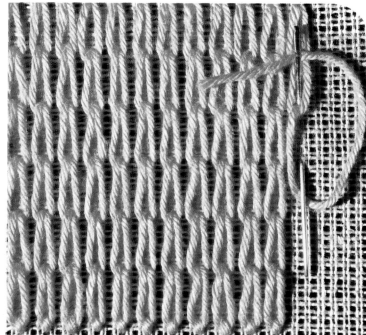

▲ *Chain stitch method 1*   ▲ *Chain stitch method 2*   ▼ *Plaited gobelin stitch*

badly. When one row is completed, finish off and start the next unless continuing in the same color, in which case turn the work and commence the next row. It is essential to finish ends securely because if they work loose a whole row of stitching will come undone.

Chain stitch method 2. Work this like ordinary chain stitch in embroidery as shown in the illustration. Finish the end of each row with a small stitch to hold the last chain in place. Once again, finish off the end of the thread securely.

Plaited gobelin. This stitch is worked in horizontal rows, over four threads up and two across to the left. Work to the length of the area you want to cover, leaving a space of two threads between each stitch. The second row is worked two threads down and in the opposite direction, giving a braided or woven effect.

▼ *Pinning muslin onto stool*   ▼ *Pattern shape pinned to canvas*   ▼ *Fitting the corner of the canvas*

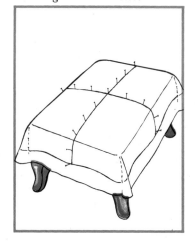

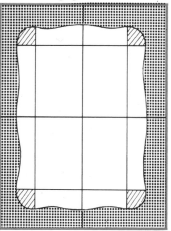

Finishing the tie-neck blouse

This chapter completes the instructions for making a tie-neck blouse, and gives tips on finishing seam allowances and hems. Another handy tip is a way to deal with sleeve openings in fine fabrics. A couture touch is added at the neckline with a snap fastener covered in matching fabric. On page 816, the subject changes completely to making a pretty terry cloth play-suit for a little girl.

Making the blouse

Stitch all the darts and press. The body and shoulder darts (if you are using them) are pressed toward the center, and the side bust darts are pressed downward. If you pressed the darts open in a soft fabric, they would fold over or wrinkle because the fabric does not have sufficient body to hold them in place during wear.

If you are using a transparent fabric, cut the depth of the darts to $\frac{3}{8}$ inch and overcast the raw edges very finely together.

Stitch the side and shoulder seams and press them open.

Trim the seam allowances evenly. To finish the raw edges, fold them under $\frac{1}{8}$ inch and whip along the folded edge (Dressmaking chapter 21, page 416).

If the fabric is transparent, press the seam allowance together toward the Front of the garment. Trim to $\frac{3}{8}$ inch and overcast as for the darts.

Finishing the Front edges

Fold each facing along the fold line to the right side of the garment, ripping the basting along the fold line.

Pin, baste and stitch along the neck edge from the marking for the collar end to the fold line.

Snip the seam allowance to allow it to follow the neckline curve (figure 1) and at the end of the stitching line where it meets the collar mark.

Turn the facing to the wrong side, baste along the stitched neck edge and press.

Pin and baste the facing firmly to the inside of the blouse along the rest of the neck edge and along the inner edge and fold line. Fold under the seam allowance on the shoulder of the facing and trim to the width of the shoulder seam on the blouse. Hand-sew to the seamline with small slip stitches.

Stitching the folded collar

Stitch the tie ends of the collar as far as the balance marks or the new marks made at the collar fitting (figure 2). If you want the

ends to be pointed, as in the photograph, taper the stitching as shown (figure 3).

Trim seams, snip off the seam allowance across the corners. Turn the tie ends to the right side, edge-baste and press.

Pin and baste the outside of the collar to the outside of the blouse, matching the Center Backs and the collar end markings on the neckline. Stitch.

Trim the seam allowance to eliminate bulk and press the seam into the collar.

Fold in the raw edge of the inside of the collar along the seamline. Hand-sew it to the stitching line to cover the seam allowance.

Pay special attention to the ends of the collar-seam, making a small bar at each end for extra strength.

Stitching on the wider collar

For the wider single tie, trim the seam allowance to $\frac{1}{4}$ inch, except where the collar is attached to the neck, on both sides of the tie. Roll the trimmed edges.

To do this, roll under the raw edges $\frac{1}{8}$ inch, then turn under again for $\frac{1}{8}$ inch and sew in place with fine slip stitches (figure 4).

Stitch on the collar as for the folded version.

The rolled sleeve opening

On finer fabrics it is not advisable to make the usual sleeve openings as shown for the fitted shirt (Dressmaking 29, p. 576). They look heavy and the very narrow seam allowance inside the facings

▼1. *Snipped neck edge of facing*

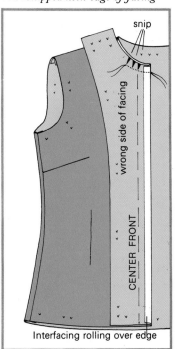

snip

wrong side of facing

CENTER FRONT

Interfacing rolling over edge

▼2. *Stitching the double tie*

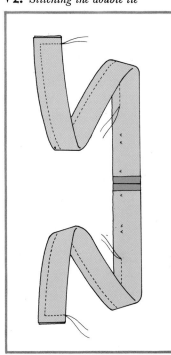

▼3. *Stitching the double tie for tapered ends*

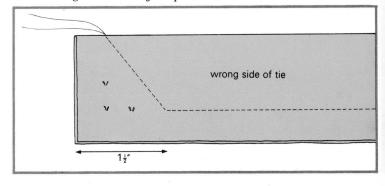

wrong side of tie

1½″

frays during wear because it cannot be double stitched. So for this soft blouse a special rolled opening is made.

First trim the seam allowance along the cuff edge of the sleeve to ½ inch.

Then measure out the opening for the roll along the cuff seamline 1 inch to each side of the opening marking.

Starting at the center of this 2 inch opening, roll the seam allowance under for ¼ inch and turn it under again by the same amount. Let it taper out into the raw edges just beyond the mark on each side.

Hand-sew the small hem firmly in position (figure **5**).

On very fine fabrics this roll should not be more than ⅛ inch deep, but do not forget to trim the whole length of the seam allowance accordingly or the ends of the cuffs will slant downward.

Finishing the sleeves

Stitch the sleeve seams, press and finish the seams.

Make the cuffs (single or double depending on your choice) as for the fitted shirt (Dressmaking chapter 29, page 576) with the extensions for link buttoning, or without if you are buttoning over. When attaching the cuffs, work across the rolled edge as shown (figure **6**).

Stitch the finished sleeves into the blouse and finish the armhole-seam edges.

If the fabric is transparent, trim the armhole seam allowance and finish as for the blouse.

The hem

A beautifully finished garment deserves a beautifully finished hem, so hand roll it.

Turn up the hem edge for ⅛ inch and then another ⅛ inch. Then, with small slip stitches, sew it to the blouse along the folded edge. Take the hem right over the front facings and do not fold them back as for the other blouses.

Stitch the ends of the hem securely and press.

Finishing

Hand-work the buttonholes (Dressmaking 19, p. 368) and stitch on the buttons. Sew on a small covered snap fastener to the top corner of the wrap so that the point will not fall back during wear.

Covering a snap fastener

To cover a snap fastener, cut two circles of fabric as shown (figure **A**) and work a gathering stitch around the outer edge of each.

Cover each half of the snap fastener by drawing up the fabric to the wrong side of it and, in the case of the ball section, piercing the ball through the center of the fabric (figure **B**). Finish off the fabric at the back and stitch on the snap fastener (figure **C**).

A.	B.	C.

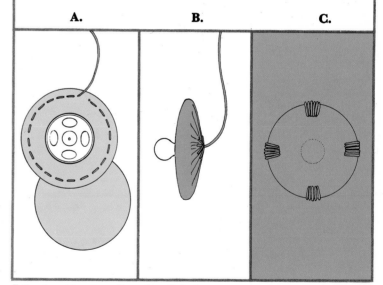

▼ **4.** *Rolling the edges of the wider tie*

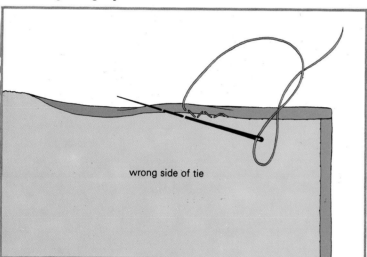

wrong side of tie

▼ **5.** *The hand-sewn rolled sleeve opening*

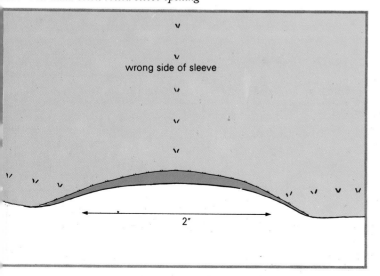

wrong side of sleeve

2″

▼ **6.** *Attaching the cuffs at the rolled edge*

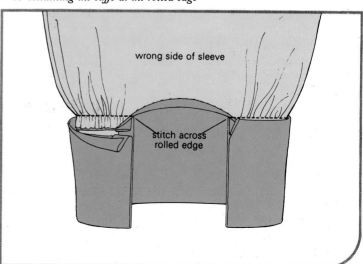

wrong side of sleeve

stitch across rolled edge

Terry cloth playsuit for a girl

The instructions given here are specifically for toweling fabrics. They include general tips on the use of toweling and on making a girl's playsuit in contrasting colors, with an attractive appliquéd pocket.

Terry cloth tips

Types of terry
There are four main types of terry cloth and they are mostly available in 36 inch to 45 inch widths.

Double-sided terry. This has loops on both sides of the fabric and most plain colors are reversible.

It is warm and cozy, but the depth of the loops makes it difficult to fasten with buttons and zippers.

Single-sided terry. Here the loops appear only on the top surface of the fabric. Garments made up in this toweling can be finished with conventional fastenings.

Stretch terry. This usually has loops on one side of the fabric.

It is particularly suitable for swimwear since it dries quickly and can be molded to the body.

Velours terry. This type has the loops on one side, sheared to form a velvety pile. The velours side is not particularly absorbent.

Cutting out
When pinning patterns on terry, do not use too many pins as pinning through thick fabric reduces the size of the pattern.

Seams in terry
The seams in toweling don't present any problem. Make ordinary seams on single terry and flat-fell seams, ½ to ¾ inch wide, for double-sided toweling, depending on the thickness of the fabric (for flat-fell seams see Dressmaking 18, page 356).

Facings in terry
Neck and armhole facings cut in toweling fabric should be avoided. Instead, bind the edges or use bias strip facings for a neat finish without bulk.

Pressing terry
When pressing terry cloth you will get a slight flattening of the loops, but if you brush over the loops with the flat of your hand while they are still warm, they will again quickly rise.

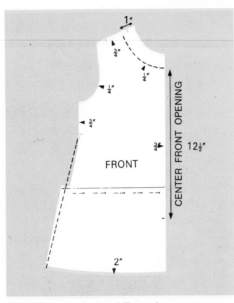

▲**1.** *The new shortened Front dress pattern*
▼**2.** *The new shortened Back dress pattern*

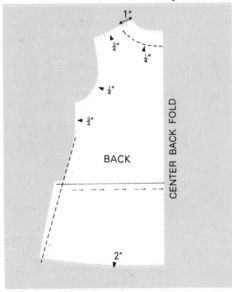

▼**3.** *Pocket hem folded outside and stitched*

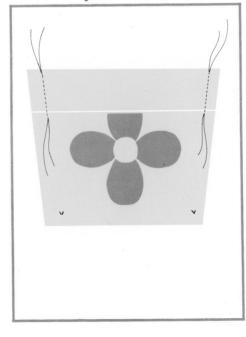

Girl's terry cloth dress

The dress pattern
This is made from the child's basic dress pattern in Dressmaking chapter 25, page 496, which comes in sizes 24, 26 and 28 inch chest. Make the Front and Back pattern pieces from the graph, altering for size as necessary.

The length. Since the beach dress is worn short with the panties showing, the basic pattern needs to be shortened.

Do not shorten it at the hemline; terry is a lot more bulky than most fabrics and it would make a very narrow garment if you did. Instead, shorten both pattern pieces by making a fold about 7 inches above the hemline to the depth desired and pin.

Then pin the Front and Back to a piece of paper, draw around the pattern pieces and straighten the side seams as shown (figures **1** and **2**). Remove the original pattern and cut out the new one.

The neckline. Lower the neckline on both the Back and Front of the new pattern by 1 inch as shown (figures **1** and **2**).

The seam allowances. The garment has a front zipper opening, so mark the Center Front to be cut with seam allowance.

Mark the Center Back to be cut on the fabric fold.

The seam allowances on the pattern vary because of the finishes used for toweling, so mark them too. Mark ¼ inch seam allowance at neckline and armhole edges and ¾ inch for other seams. Also mark a 2 inch hem allowance. This will act as a reminder when making the garment, as it is difficult to tailor's tack toweling fabrics.

The pocket and daisy patterns
The bucket-shaped pocket is another type of patch pocket.

Trace the pocket pattern on page 818 and cut out. Trace and cut out separate patterns for the daisy petals and center.

To find the position for the pocket on the dress, place the pocket pattern on the Front pattern piece ¼ inch up from the hem and with the upper edge 1½ inches from the Center Front. Draw around it.

If the hem is slightly curved, tilt the pattern so that it is even with the hemline and check the position at the fitting stage.

Yardages and notions
To find the amount of fabric needed, make a layout on paper the same width as the toweling, using the Back, Front and daisy petal pieces. The pockets and daisy centers are cut from contrasting fabric.

Allow for seam and hem allowances. Also allow for three bias strips to finish the neck and armhole edges. These should be

4 times the width of the finished rouleau, plus ⅛ inch.

If the fabric you choose has a one way design, make allowance for this when calculating the yardage.

Draw around the pattern shapes so that you can use the paper as a layout at the cutting stage.

You will also need a 12 inch zipper and matching thread.

Cutting out
Lay out the pattern using your paper layout as a guide. Do not forget to place the Back on a fold and cut the Center Front with seam allowance.

Mark all the seam and hem allowances with pin lines except for the daisy, which has no seam allowance. Cut out. Also cut out the three bias strips.

Cut out 2 pocket shapes and 2 daisy centers from the contrast fabric.

Marking the pattern details
Tailor's tack only where it is absolutely necessary, such as at balance marks, darts (if you are using them), and seam ends. Also mark the pocket positions with single tailor's tacks through slits made in the dress pattern.

Mark the end of the opening for the zipper in the Center Front 12½ inches from the neck edge.

Don't mark the seamlines, but keep the pattern at hand and measure them out as you stitch the garment.

Fitting
Pin and baste the dress for fitting and make any necessary corrections.

Inserting the zipper
Stitch the Center Front seam below the opening mark, then baste the opening together. Finish the seam allowance and press the seam open.

Insert the zipper using the straight seam method (Dressmaking chapter 8, page 156), but sew it by hand with small firm backstitches. Stitching by machine will make the surface loops tilt in opposite directions.

Sew the zipper to the seam allowance with felling stitches.

Making the pockets
Pin and baste the daisy petals onto each pocket piece, working very close to the edges and using a matching sewing thread. If you have a zigzag on your machine, follow the instructions for appliqué in the machine manual, but engage a slightly larger stitch width to appliqué the daisy. For hand appliqué use a closely worked overcasting stitch in matching sewing or embroidery thread, catching through all

Girl's beach playsuit made in colorful terry cloth with daisy petal pockets

layers of fabric.

Appliqué the daisy centers the same way. Press the appliqué, then finish the pockets. Fold the 1½ inch hem allowance at the top to the outside of each pocket and stitch at the sides as shown (figure 3).

Overcast the raw edge, turn the hem to the inside and sew by hand.

Fold under the remaining seam allowance and baste.

Position the pockets on the dress. Pin, baste and topstitch close to the edge. Press.

Finishing the dress
Pin, baste and stitch the side and shoulder seams, overcast the raw edges and press the seams. Also stitch the darts if used.

Using the bias strips, bind the neck and armholes as for the basic dress.

Finish the hem in the usual way and give the garment a final pressing.

Girl's terry panties

The pattern
The pattern on the next two pages will fit a 30 inch hip and corresponds to the largest dress size. Instructions for making the pattern smaller follow.

Trace the Front and Back pattern pieces. The tracing will only give you half a Front and Back, so you will need to complete the pattern pieces for an open layout.

Making the pattern smaller
To shorten. Measure the child through the crotch from Center Front to Center Back and compare the measurement on the pattern.

Divide the difference by 4 and deduct this amount equally from the waist and the depth of the crotch on both Back and Front pattern pieces.

To make narrower. If the child's hips are less than 30 inches, deduct the difference in equal amounts from the centers and side seams of both Back and Front pattern pieces until you have the correct width.

Yardages and notions

To find out the amount of toweling needed, make a layout on paper as for the dress. If you are making the dress as well, include the pocket and daisy center patterns in this layout.

As you can see by the straight of grain marking, the panties are cut in the cross of the fabric to give maximum comfort during wear.

You will also need 1 package of bias binding, ¼in elastic to fit the waist and legs, and matching thread.

Cutting out and marking

Using your paper layout, cut out the fabric and mark the pattern details as for the dress.

Making the panties

The seams. Because the panties are cut on the cross, ordinary seams will tend to curl, so an open flat-fell seam is used with zigzag stitching.

With right sides facing, stitch the side and crotch seams, using a shallow zigzag. Press the seam allowance to one side.

Trim the inside seam allowance as for flat-fell seaming (Dressmaking chapter 18) and trim the top seam for a flat-fell, but without the allowance for the turning.

Generally these seams should be as narrow as possible, but to make allowance for towelings which fray, leave ¼ inch on the inside and ⅜ inch on the top.

Then, using a small zigzag setting, work over the raw edge of the double seam allowance to make the open flat-fell. If you don't have a zigzag on your machine, make ordinary flat-fell seams.

The waist and leg casings. Finish the raw edge of the seam allowance at the waist.

Turn the waist seam allowance to the inside and stitch in place with the same zigzag setting, or, if you are using a straight stitch, turn under the edge first. Don't forget to leave an opening in the seam to insert the elastic.

To make the casings at the leg edges, finish them with bias binding.

With right sides facing, raw edges even, stitch one edge of the binding around the leg edges. Turn the binding completely to the inside and machine stitch the other edge in place, finishing the ends.

Slot elastic into the waist and leg casings to finish.

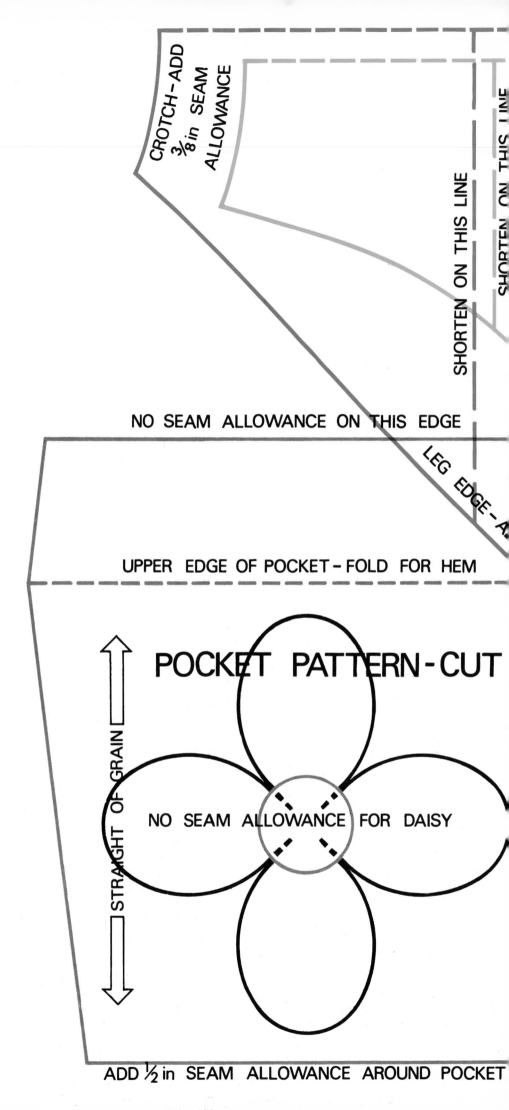

PANTIES PATTERN

FRONT —— CUT 1
BACK —— CUT 1

SIZE: 30in HIP

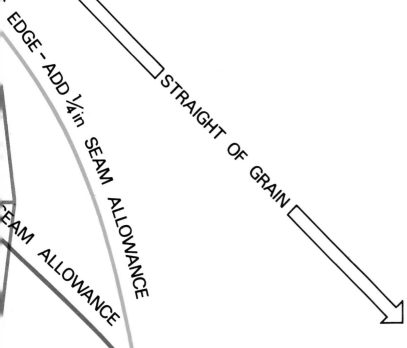

EDGE - ADD ¼in SEAM ALLOWANCE

EAM ALLOWANCE

STRAIGHT OF GRAIN

WAISTLINE – SHORTEN HERE – ADD ¾ in SEAM ALLOWANCE

SIDE-SEAM-ADD ⅜in SEAM ALLOWANCE

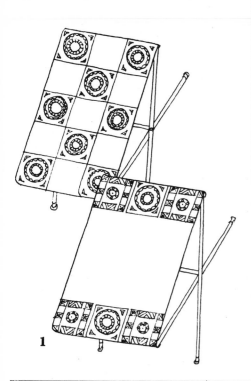

1

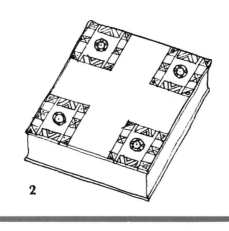

2

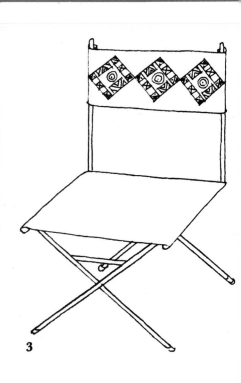

3

Squares and circles are good, simple shapes to build designs on and the ones shown here are typical examples. These, and similar designs of your own, can be used in a variety of techniques wherever embroidery is wanted.

Squares and circles

1. *Brighten up plain, folding garden stools with embroidery.*
2. *Box pillows can be useful for sitting around the house Japanese-style. Embroider them to match the chairs or stools.*
3. *Give an embroidery face lift to the back of a garden chair.*

Pattern Library

Color explosion

Color is fun, especially when you experiment with several tones of any color. In this design, colors explode away from the center, becoming lighter and held in a fairly strong border. Six-strand floss colors are available in as many as eleven tones of a single color, but this particular design uses only four tones of each shade. They are DMC 6-strand floss in red Nos. 355, 760, 761 and 945; blue Nos. 312, 322 and 3325 with white; and old gold Nos. 732, 733, 3013 and 822.

Knitting in the round

Sweaters, socks, stockings, gloves, mittens, skirts and many other garments can be worked on sets of needles, producing a tubular, seamless piece of work. This does not mean that there cannot be shaping with carefully planned increasing and decreasing calculated to give the required shape.

Knitting in rounds also aids the knitter because the right side of the work is always facing, which helps when working complicated or multi-colored patterns. It is for this reason, in fact, that Fair Isle knitters use the method, even in sweaters with long sleeves. Instead of stopping at armhole level, a tube is worked the whole length of the sweater up to the shoulder. From the armhole level upward, the yarn is wound around the needle several times in a line where the armhole is required. On the next round, the previous loops are dropped and the process repeated. This gives a ladder of strands on either side which is cut when the work is completed, each end being darned back into the fabric. The stitches for the sleeves are then picked up around the armhole and the sleeves knitted in rounds down to the wrist.

This method is both quick and practical, since it is a simple matter to add or lengthen cuffs at any time.

Casting on with more than two needles

The actual casting on of each stitch is exactly as normal; however, because there are more needles to be considered, there are two methods of working. No matter how many needles are being used—and for a large sweater you may require five or six—one is used for knitting and the total number of stitches is divided between the remaining needles. You can either cast on the number of stitches required on the first needle, then proceed to the second and so on, or you can cast on the total number onto one needle and then slip them onto the other needles. The second method is perhaps the easier because it is less likely to cause the cast-on edge to become twisted.

Form the needles into a circle and slip the spare needle into the first stitch on the first needle. If you now knit this stitch, taking the yarn directly to it from the last stitch, the circle you require is formed. Continue to knit all the stitches on the first needle. Once the needle is free of stitches, knit along the second needle. Continue in this way. This is all there is to round knitting. Because the right side of the work is always facing you, every round produces stockinette stitch and not garter stitch, as would be the case when working back and forth in rows. Garter stitch is made by working one round knit and one round purl alternately.

Because it is easy to lose track of the beginning of a round, the simplest method of marking it is to slip a knotted loop of contrasting yarn onto the needle before the first stitch of a round. Simply slip this loop onto the right-hand needle, without knitting it, on every round, and the beginning of a round can be seen at a glance.

More than one marker may be required because the pattern may

include shapings at either side of a point where a side seam would be placed, or down the back seam of a stocking. If you are working a gored skirt, it may be easier to mark each gore with a loop of one color and use a second color to mark the actual round beginning.

Future chapters deal with details of shaping when knitting in the round, discussing such areas as the thumb and fingers of gloves and turning the heels of socks and stockings. The illustrations given here show how a neat, mock seam effect can be achieved with correct shaping on the leg of a sock and how shaping in graduated panels can produce a swinging gored skirt. This paneled effect is ideal for a full-skirted dress where considerable bulk needs to be reduced before beginning the bodice.

Try a simple sock pattern and you will see how easy knitting in the round can be, particularly when it comes to finishing.

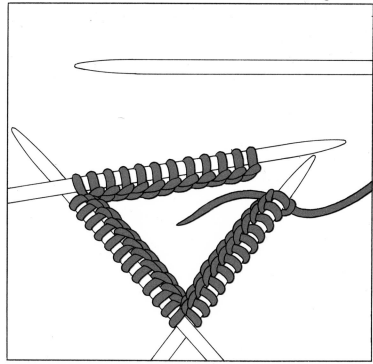

▲ *Casting on with 3 needles*   ▼ *Joining casting on with the 4th needle*

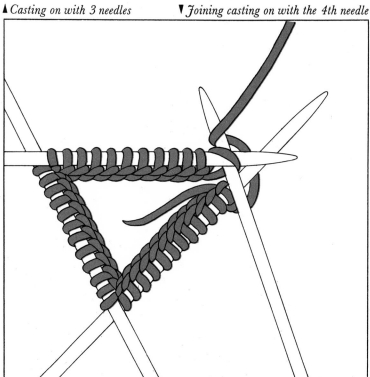

▲ *Casting on with 4 needles*
▼ *Shaping on the back of a sock*

▲ *Joining casting on with the 5th needle*
▼ *Long socks and short socks, with plain or intricate patterns, can be knitted in rounds*

▲ *Shaping at either side of a mock seam*

Party time dress and cardigan

Basic Wardrobe Knitting

This dainty dress, tied with ribbons on the shoulders, will delight any little girl. Paired with a long-sleeved cardigan, it's perfect for summertime special occasions.

Sizes

Directions are for 22in chest. The figures in brackets [ ] refer to the 24 and 26in sizes respectively.
Cardigan Length down center back, $9\frac{1}{2}[10\frac{3}{4}:12]$in, adjustable. Sleeve seam, $7\frac{1}{4}[8\frac{1}{4}:9\frac{1}{2}]$in, adjustable.
Dress Skirt length, $8\frac{1}{2}[9\frac{3}{4}:10\frac{3}{4}]$in, adjustable.

Gauge

$7\frac{1}{2}$ sts and $9\frac{1}{2}$ rows to 1in over stockinette stitch worked on No.3 needles.

Materials

Sports yarn (2oz skeins)
Cardigan 2[2:3] skeins of main color A
1 skein of contrast color B
Dress 4[4:5] skeins of main color A
1 skein of contrast color B
One pair No.2 needles (or Canadian No.11)
One pair No.3 needles (or Canadian No.10)
Three small pearl buttons
One yard 1in wide ribbon

Cardigan back

Using No.2 needles and A, cast on 85[93:101] sts. Work $1\frac{1}{2}[1\frac{1}{2}:1\frac{3}{4}]$in K1, P1 rib, ending with a RS row.
Next row K to form ridge.
Change to No.3 needles.
Beg with a K row, continue in st st until work measures $5[5\frac{3}{4}:7]$in from beg or desired length to underarm, ending with a P row. **

Shape armholes

Bind off 2[3:4] sts at beg of next 2 rows, 2 sts at beg of next 4 rows, and 1 st at beg of next 2[4:6] rows.
Continue without shaping until armholes measure $4[4\frac{1}{4}:4\frac{1}{2}]$in, ending with P row.

Shape shoulders

Bind off 8 sts at beg of next 4 rows; then 6[7:8] sts beg of next 2 rows.
Bind off rem sts.

Left front

Using No.2 needles and A, cast on 38[42:46] sts.

Work as given for back to **, ending at armhole edge.

Shape armholes and front edge

Bind off at arm edge 2[3:4] sts; then 2 sts every other row twice and 1 st once 1[2:3] times; *at the same time*, dec one st on next and every 4th row at center front edge until 22[23:24] sts rem.
Continue without shaping until armhole measures same as back to shoulder, ending at armhole edge.

Shape shoulder

At arm edge, bind off 8 sts every other row twice; then 6[7:8] sts once.

Right front

Work as given for left front, reversing all shaping.

Sleeves

Using No.2 needles and A, cast on 43[45:47] sts. Work rib as given for back.
Change to No.3 needles.
Next row K to form ridge.
Next row K to end, inc 5 sts evenly across row. 48[50:52] sts.
Beg with a P row, continue in st st, inc one st at each end of 10th and every following 10th row until there are 58[62:66] sts.
Continue without shaping until sleeve measures $7\frac{1}{4}[8\frac{1}{4}:9\frac{1}{2}]$in from beg or desired length to underarm, ending with a P row.

Shape cap

Bind off 3[4:5] sts at beg of next 2 rows, then 3[4:5] sts once, 3 sts every other row 4 times and 2 sts every other row 10[12:14] times. Bind off rem sts.

Front border

Join shoulder seams. Using No. 2 needles and A, pick up and K178[194:214] sts evenly around neck edge from cast-on edge of right front to cast-on edge of left front.
***P 1 row. K 1 row. P 1 row.

Change to 2-color patt.
st row K2 B, *2A, 2B,
ep from * to end.
nd row P2 A, *2B, 2A,
ep from * to end.
rd row (buttonhole row)
Using A, K8, *bind off 2 sts,
K16[18:22], rep from * once,
ind off 2, K to end.
th row With B, P to end
asting on 2 sts over those
ound off on previous row.
th row K2 A, *2B, 2A,
ep from * to end.
th row P2 B, *2A, 2B, rep
rom * to end.
K 1 row. P 1 row. K 2 rows.
Using A only and beg with a
K row, work 11 rows st st,
vorking buttonholes as
efore on 5th and 6th rows.
Bind off. ***

Dress
(Front and Back alike)

Using No.3 needles and A,
ast on 150[166:182] sts.
K 16 rows garter st.
Beg with a K row work 4
ows st st.
Change to 2-color patt.
st row K2 B, *2A, 2B,
ep from * to end.
nd row P2 A, *2B, 2A, rep
rom * to end.
rd row Using A, K to end.
th row Using A, P to end.
th row K2 A, *2B, 2A, rep
rom * to end.
th row P2 B, *2A, 2B,
ep from * to end.
Using A only, K 1 row, P 1
ow, K 2 rows.
Beg with a K row, continue
n st st until skirt measures
$1\frac{1}{2}$[$9\frac{3}{4}$:$10\frac{3}{4}$]in from beg or
lesired length, ending
vith a K row.
Next row (P2 tog 4 times,
P1) 8 times, P2 tog 3[11:19]
imes, (P1, P2 tog 4 times)
8 times. 83[91:99] sts.
Work $1\frac{1}{4}$[$1\frac{1}{2}$:$1\frac{1}{2}$]in K1, P1
ib, ending with a WS row.
Beg with a K row, continue
n st st on bodice for
$3\frac{3}{4}$[2:$2\frac{1}{2}$]in, ending with a
P row.

Shape armholes
At each arm edge, bind off 2
3[3:4] sts; then 2 sts at beg
of next 12 rows. Dec 1 st each
end every row 24[26:28]

▲ *A matching cardigan to wear with the prettily ribboned party dress on the opposite page*

times (32 sts). K 12 rows garter
st on rem sts. Bind off.

Armbands

Join side seams. Using No.2
needles and A, cast on 16 sts
for strap; using same needle,
pick up and K88[92:96] sts
evenly around armhole, turn
and cast on 16 sts for other
end of strap.
Work from *** to *** as
given for cardigan border,
omitting buttonholes.

Finishing

Cardigan Fold border in
half to WS and sl st in place.
Work buttonhole st around
both thicknesses of buttonholes.
Join side and sleeve seams.
Sew in sleeves.
Sew on buttons to correspond
with buttonholes.

Dress. Fold armbands in
half to WS and sl st in
place, joining cast-on and
bound-off edges of straps tog.
Sew ribbon ties to each end
of straps.

Net results in filet crochet

Filet lace is one of the most interesting forms of crochet and its uses are numerous. Worked in fine cotton, it makes beautiful and long-wearing net curtains. In thicker yarn, filet crochet can be used to make anything from a pretty bedspread to a fashionable sweater. This chapter describes how to work a mesh ground—a fabric of spaces joined by doubles—and includes a chart for filet crochet.

Mesh ground

This consists of a group of spaces joined by doubles made by working *ch2, skip 2ch, 1dc, rep from * for required length, ending with 1dc. The next and following rows are worked in the same way, working the doubles into the doubles of the previous row.

Beginning with a block

To begin the first row with a block of doubles make 3 extra chains to stand as the first double and make next double in the 4th chain from hook. Complete first block of 4 doubles by working 1 double in each of the next 2 chains.

Beginning with a space

To begin the first row with a space, make 5 extra chains of which the first 3 chains stand as the first double. Then work 1 double in the 8th chain from hook.

Beginning with a block of doubles

If the row begins with a block over a block of doubles, without increases or decreases, turn work, chain 3 to stand as first double, skip first double and work 1 double into next 3 doubles, or required number of doubles to complete block.

▲ Mesh ground of doubles and spaces
▼ Sample beginning with a block of doubles

▲ Beginning with a block of doubles
▼ Sample of alternating doubles and spaces

▲ Beginning with a space
▼ Making mesh ground beginning with a space

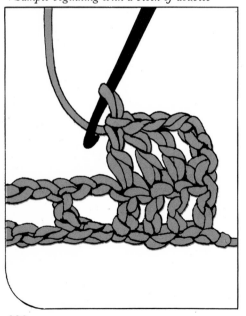
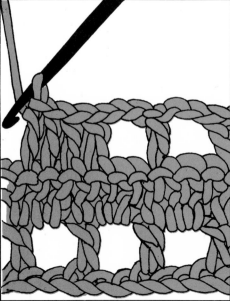

Beginning with alternating doubles and spaces

If the row begins with a block of doubles over a space, chain 3 to stand as first double, *work 2 double into space of previous row, 1 double into next double, rep from * to end. If the row begins with a space over a block of doubles, chain 5, skip 3 doubles and work 1 double into last double of block. Vary blocks of doubles and spaces as pattern requires.

Mesh ground of doubles and spaces

If the row begins with a space over a space, without increases or decreases, turn work, chain 5 and work 1 double into 2nd double of previous row.

Sample of filet crochet

Working methods of filet crochet are very often given by means of a chart, but unlike knitting, each square on the chart does not necessarily represent just one stitch. A chart and row by row directions are given for this sample so that you may become familiar with this method. In this case, each open square on the chart represents a chain 2 space plus a connecting double, and each cross represents a block of 2 doubles plus a connecting double. Begin at the bottom right-hand corner of the chart for the 1st row,

turn work and read from left to right for the 2nd row, and so on. Ch50.

1st row. Work 1dc into 8th ch from hook (standing as first dc and first ch2 space), *ch2, skip 2ch, 1dc into next ch, rep from * to end. Turn. (15 spaces.)

2nd row. Ch5 (standing as first dc and first ch2 space), skip ch2 space, 1dc into next dc, 2dc into next ch2 space, 1dc into next dc, 2dc into next ch2 space, 1dc into next dc, (2 blocks), ch2, skip ch2 space, 1dc into next dc, (1 space), (2dc into ch2 space, 1dc into dc) twice, (ch2, skip ch2 space, 1dc into dc) 3 times, (2dc into ch2 space, 1dc into dc) twice, ch2, skip ch2, 1dc into top of 3rd turning ch. Turn.

3rd row. Ch5, skip 1dc and 2ch, 1dc into next dc, 2 blocks over next 2 blocks working 1dc into each dc, 1 space over 1 space, ch2, skip 2dc, 1dc into dc, (1 space over 1 block), 1dc into each of next 3dc, 2dc into ch2 space, 1dc into 1dc, (1 block over 1 space), 1 space over 1 space, 2dc into ch2 space, 1dc into 1 dc, 1dc into each of next 3dc, (1 block over 1 space, 1 block over 1 block), 1 space over 1 block, 1 space over 1 space, 2 blocks over 2 blocks, ch2, skip 2ch, 1dc into 3rd of turning ch. Turn.

Continue working in this way from the chart, noting that 14 rows form one complete pattern repeat.

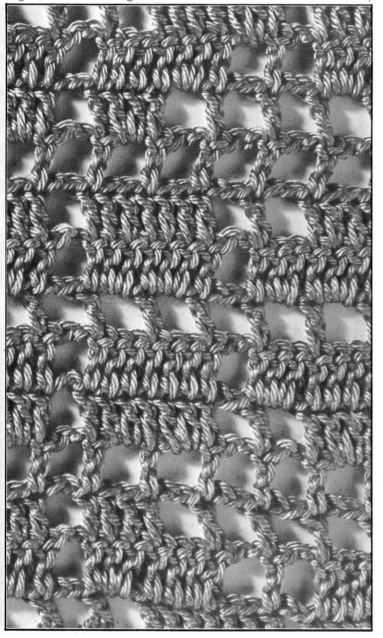

▲ *Chart for filet crochet pattern*
◄ *Part of the filet crochet pattern worked from directions and chart*
▼ *The filet crochet pattern makes a pretty dressing table runner*

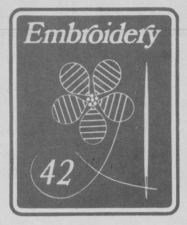

A nosegay of summer daisies

Flowers embroidered on gingham give a refreshing new look to furnishings, the softness of the design contrasting with the fabric background. Make this gay daisy-embroidered pillow to brighten a bedroom, to add a splash of color to a family or sun room, or for a set of garden chairs.

Materials you will need
- ☐ ½yd 36in wide gingham
- ☐ Pillow form 14in by 14in (finished pillow 13in by 13in)
- ☐ 10in zipper
- ☐ Crewel needle size 7
- ☐ Six-strand floss, 1 skein each dark yellow and bright green; 2 skeins each lemon yellow and brown; 6 skeins white

Stitches and threads
The stitches used in this design are outline stitch, chain stitch, long and short stitch, French knots and Romanian stitch. The entire design is worked in six-strand floss using a varying number of strands for the different parts.

Transferring the design
First cut the fabric down the center fold and mark the center of one piece vertically and horizontally with lines of basting. Transfer the design by the tracing method (see Embroidery chapter 4, page 68), centering it on the fabric.

Working the design
Flowers. The petals on the flowers are embroidered in long and short stitch using three strands of floss. The outlines of the petals are worked in outline stitch with two strands. Some of the petals on each flower can be stitched using five strands of floss to give a raised look.
Buds. Some of the buds are embroidered with brown and the rest with bright green, using four strands of floss. The edges of the buds are in outline stitch and filled with long and short stitch.
Bud petals. The petals on the buds are worked with two chain stitches, a small one inside a larger one, using four strand of floss.
Stems. Work the stems in outline stitch in brown and green alternately, using four strands of floss. The stems are caught together with three Romanian stitches in yellow.
Centers. The centers of the daisies are first worked in outline stitch, working the outer edge of the circle first and working in to the center. Then several French knots are made over the outline stitch.

To make the pillow
When all the embroidery is complete, press carefully on the wrong side and trim the fabric to the size of the pillow, plus ⅝ inch seam allowances all around. Make the pillow according to the instructions in Embroidery chapter 18, page 348, leaving a 10 inch opening for inserting the zipper.

The outline of the design to trace for the pillow

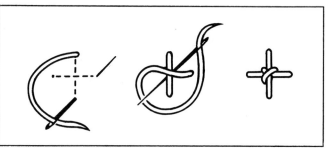

Four-legged knot stitch

When the second stitch of the cross is made, a coral stitch knots it firmly in position. Then the fourth leg is completed. This stitch can be used as a powdered filling.

Raised knot or square boss stitch

A backstitch is worked over each arm of the cross to make a firm raised knot.

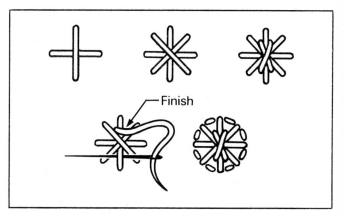

—Finish

Star stitch

A useful stitch, often arranged as a powdered filling. For backstitched star, both the backstitch and the central cross can be worked in a contrasting thread.

American patchwork quilt

American patchwork is often closer to appliqué work than traditional English patchwork, while its characteristic quilted background gives American patchwork much of its charm. The patchwork shapes derive from English and Dutch patchwork and also from colonial America itself. One of the most famous of the latter is the princess feather, as illustrated in figure 1, which is thought to have been inspired by the feathered headdresses of Indian princesses.

▼1. *An American quilt using the princess feather and star patterns*

The star is another traditional American pattern with considerable variations on the basic shape. Two stars are given here—the pointed star and the round star, both of which, like the princess feather, are large motifs and should be used in a lively, informal way.

Assembling the pointed star

A section of this pattern is given full size as a tracing pattern (figure 2). You will need 8 of these pieces and 4 of them must be reversed. The pieces are joined together as in traditional patchwork and then overcast to the background. The assembled star is shown in figure 3.

Assembling the rounded star

A section of this pattern is again given full size (figure 4). You will need 8 pieces and 4 of them must be reversed. They are joined together along the straight edges as shown in figure 5.

Making your own quilt

American quilts do not reach to the ground but lie on top of the bed as a coverlet. An average single bed size quilt should measure about 62in by 100in and a double bed size quilt about 80in by 100in.

You will need:

☐ Background fabric in a neutral color or a color which echoes one of the colors you will use in the patchwork. For the best results choose a firm, closely woven, heavyweight cotton.
It is possible to use readymade cotton quilting for the background fabric, but the patchwork design and quilting should complement each other either in color or shape.
☐ Basting thread
☐ Brown paper

Fold the background into quarters and mark the fold lines with basting.

Decide which patchwork shape you will use for the design and cut out several patterns of each complete motif in brown paper. Arrange a quarter of the design using the paper patterns in one of the marked-off quarters of the background fabric. When this looks right—and only the designer of the quilt can tell this—mark the placing for the motifs with further basting. Mark the other quarters in the same way.

Making the patchwork

You will need:

☐ Patterned and colored fabrics for the patches
☐ Matching sewing thread
☐ A fine needle
☐ Sandpaper (medium-coarse)
☐ Scissors to cut the sandpaper
☐ Scissors to cut the fabric
☐ Basting thread

Draw or trace the shapes you have chosen onto the smooth side of the sandpaper. Cut out the sandpaper shapes and place them rough side down onto the fabric. The sandpaper will cling to the fabric and help you to cut accurately. Unless you wish to center a particular part of a patterned fabric, place the sandpaper on the wrong side of the fabric as it may be too abrasive for delicate fibers.

Cut accurately around the edge of each sandpaper pattern leaving $\frac{1}{4}$ inch seam allowance. Remove the sandpaper and turn the seam allowance to the wrong side of each patch. Baste the edges down carefully.

Press well using a pressing cloth.

Assemble all the motifs now, so that the patchwork is ready to be applied to the background.

Assembling the cover

You will need:

☐ The marked-up background fabric
☐ Basting thread
☐ Sewing thread to match the patches
☐ Prepared patchwork
☐ Lining fabric (the same amount as the background fabric). This should be non-

slip, medium-weight, with the color matched to the background fabric

Baste the assembled patchwork onto the background fabric in the design you have chosen. Sew the patchwork down with tiny overcasting stitches, keeping it as flat as possible.

When the patchwork is sewed down, remove all the basting threads and press the work carefully.

Place the lining onto the finished cover, right sides together, and stitch around the edges leaving a long opening on one side. Turn the cover right side out through the opening and close with overcasting stitches. Catch the lining fabric to the background fabric all over, with tiny stitches at about 5 inch intervals.

Interlining. Traditionally American patchwork quilts were made warmer by the addition of extra layers of fabric (old blankets, sheets or quilt batting) placed between the background fabric and the lining. You can follow tradition or dispense with an interlining altogether. On the other hand, if you are using ready-made quilting, the interlining is already built-in. Even so, the quilting will still need to be lined.

Quilting the cover

These instructions do not apply to ready-made quiltings.

The quilting may be done on a machine with a simple straight stitch or by hand. If you work by hand, use tiny running stitches, using a stabbing technique to be sure that all layers are caught together.

In both cases, use a thread to match the background fabric and work the quilting from the middle of the cover toward the edges.

Make rows of stitches through all the layers in patterned lines around the patchwork. The quilting should echo the pattern of the patchwork but can be quite freely expressed. Figure **6** shows a good example of this.

6. *A traditional star with the quilted background echoing the star shape* ►

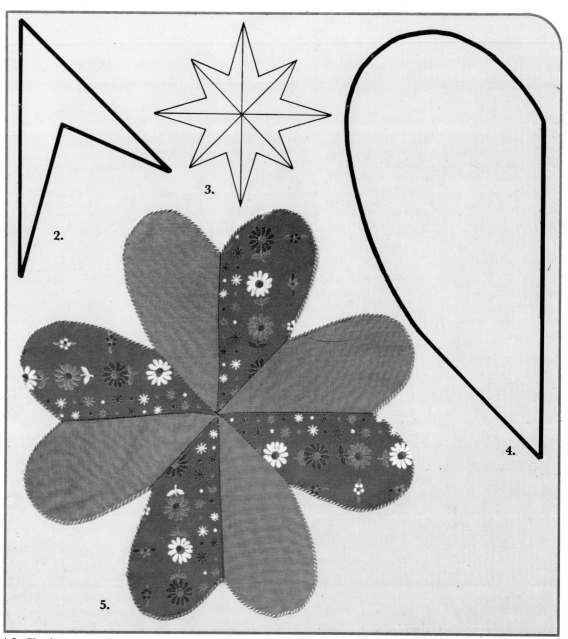

▲**2.** *Tracing pattern for a section of the pointed star*　**3.** *The pointed star assembled*　**4.** *Tracing pattern for a section of the rounded star*　**5.** *The rounded star assembled*

The shirt dress story

The shirt dress is a true fashion classic, remaining with us through all the style changes that fashion designers have created. Season after season, the shirt dress reappears in new shapes and forms. Fabric, color and detailing all combine to give the impression of variety although the basic style remains the same. Take the styles illustrated here—they are all simple variations of the shirt dress, but each has a completely different look—all made from the patterns in the Creative Hands Pattern Pack given in Volume 22.

Instructions are given for four of these versions, starting in this chapter. They are: A. the button-down shirt dress with shirt collar and cuffs; B. the shirt dress with collar band finish; C. the evening shirt dress with tab fastening and D. the shirt dress with full bishop sleeves.

Although the instructions deal specifically with these versions, all the details are interchangeable and can be combined with garments from previous chapters to give you the full range of styles featured here. You can apply some of the techniques to commercial paper patterns as well.

So you see, all you need for a distinctive wardrobe is a basic set of patterns and a lively fashion sense.

Suitable fabrics

There simply isn't a fabric which has not been used to make the shirt dress. You can make it in a lightweight knit or a crisp cotton for summer, warmer and heavier fabrics for winter, and more sophisticated fabrics for cocktail or evening wear.

Here is a list to help you decide:

For summer wear: eyelet embroidery; gingham; cotton and man-made fiber mixtures; cotton knit.

For winter wear: most fine woolen dress-weight fabrics; cotton and wool mixtures such as Viyella; wool jersey; man-made fiber knits; fine tweeds.

For evening wear: all types of fine or medium-weight silks; voile; organdy; brocade and embroidered fabrics; some firm crêpes.

Ideas and variations

Four versions are given in detail. These have been selected because they entail a number of pattern adaptations, but you don't have to stop there.

Pockets. Go on by adding pockets to the button-down version. Topstitch the pockets in position and then topstitch the edges of the dress to match.

Sleeves. Another style could be created using the roll-up short sleeve pattern given in Dressmaking chapter 18, page 356.

Many woman like a ¾ length sleeve and this can easily be made by shortening the long shirt sleeve. But don't forget to make the cuffs larger as they have to encircle a larger part of the arm. If you want to link button the cuffs for ¾ length sleeves, it is best to make the links with hat elastic so that they will not be too tight.

B.   A.

D.

C.

The straight shirt dress. This is another version you can make. Just straighten the side seams from the hipline down and do away with the flare. Remember that the hemline will be tighter and the buttons on the button-down version will have to withstand a lot more strain.

Embroidery and beads. To decorate a plain silk shirt dress for evening wear, embroider the collar and cuffs with beads and paillettes. Choose the plastic variety which are lightweight and will not make the collar points flop.

Belts. Belts can also make a change, but avoid the stiff and tightly buckled ones. They are meant to be worn over fitted waists and a dress cut without a waist seam would gather up under them.

A. The button-down shirt dress

This version has a button-down front, a shirt collar and shirt sleeves.

The pattern

You will need the following pattern pieces from the Creative Hands Pattern Pack: from the dress pattern sheet, the Front and Back pattern pieces, numbers 1 and 2; from the accessory pattern sheet, the long shirt sleeve, shirt collar, collar band and cuff pattern pieces, numbers 8, 10, 11 and 12.

The Front. To adapt the pattern for the button-down dress, first make a new pattern.

Pin the Front pattern piece securely on a piece of paper with the Center Front 1 inch from the straight edge of the paper. Draw around the edges with a pencil and extend the hem and necklines to the edge of the paper.

The 1 inch margin between the pattern and paper edge on the new pattern is the Center Front wrap for the button fastening (figure 1).

Cut out the new Front pattern.

Space out the positions for the eleven buttonholes on the Center Front line of the new Front pattern as shown in figure 1.

You will have one buttonhole in the collar band, so allow equal spacing between the first buttonhole on the dress Front and that on the collar band.

Leave a complete buttonhole distance between the hemline and the last button and do not try to work a buttonhole through the turned up hem.

The front facing. Copy the neck, shoulder and front edges of the Front pattern and measure out the front facing as shown (figure 1). The facing is 4 inches wide

836

along the Front and hem edge and 2 inches wide at the shoulderline.

Cut out the front facing pattern.

Yardages

54in width. Without one way—sizes 32½, 34 and 36, 2⅝ yards; size 38, 2⅞ yards; sizes 40 and 42, 3⅛ yards.

54in width. With one way—size 32½, 2⅝ yards; size 34, 2¾ yards; size 36, 3⅛ yards; sizes 38, 40 and 42, 3¼ yards.

36in width. Without one way—size 32½, 4 yards; size 34, 4⅛ yards; size 36, 4⅜ yards; sizes 38, 40 and 42, 4½ yards.

36in width. With one way—size 32½, 4 yards; size 34, 4¼ yards; size 36, 4⅜ yards; size 38, 4½ yards; sizes 40 and 42, 5 yards.

Notions

You will need:
- ☐ 14 small buttons (2 extra for link buttoned cuffs)
- ☐ Matching thread
- ☐ Interfacing (see below), the length of the shoulder to hem plus ¾ inch seam allowance

Hints on interfacing

Unlike the shirt blouse, the Center Front edge of the dress needs interfacing.

The best type to use is a soft pre-shrunk cotton lawn. It is available in different colors, so choose one to match the fabric you are using. This will stop the interfacing creating shading through the top fabric.

If you want to make the dress in a sheer fabric and have a good fabric store near you, you may be able to obtain pure silk organza for an interfacing. This is so colorless that it can be used for the sheerest fabrics. Otherwise, ask at the store for the right kind of interfacing for your particular fabric.

If you find that the interfacing shows through and changes the color of the fabric, it is best not to use it, as long as the fabric has enough substance to support itself. If not, don't use that particular fabric to make the shirt dress.

It is always best to buy and try fabric and interfacing at the same time. This way you will avoid being committed to an unsuitable fabric.

Lining the shirt dress

Lining the button-down shirt dress is not easy or advisable, even if the fabric is mounted straight onto the lining. In washable dresses, a lining makes ironing very difficult. You also lose the shirt-like feel of the fabric and it becomes bulky.

Cutting and marking

Choose the appropriate layout for your style, size and fabric width from the layouts

included in this chapter.

Fold the fabric as shown on the layout. If you are working on a large area of a lightweight fabric, pin the selvages and fold lightly. This will prevent the fabric from rolling out of the correct fold, which could result in your cutting the sides unevenly without even noticing it.

Note: The collar and collar band are cut in the same grain of the fabric.

Remember, the pattern has no hem or seam allowance, so add ¾ inch for seams all around and 2½ inches for the hem.

Cut out the dress, mark the pattern details and remove the pattern pieces.

Cut out the Front, collar, collar band and cuff interfacings as you need them.

Fitting

Baste the dress, including sleeves and cuffs together for fitting and make any necessary alterations.

For the fitting it is best to baste the Center Front seam from hip level to hem.

Making the Center Fronts

Having ascertained the correct length of the dress when fitting, cut out two front interfacing pieces using the front facing pattern. You will not need seam allowance along the inner edge or a hem allowance.

Pin the interfacing to the inside of both dress Fronts.

Baste in position with two rows of basting stitches, the first just outside the seam lines, and the second about ¾ inch in from the inner edge so that you can work on it later.

Pin and baste the facings to the right side of the dress.

Stitch in place along the seamlines of the Front wrap—that is, from the neck edge down to the hem.

Layer the seam allowance by trimming as follows: Trim the interfacing to ⅛ inch, the facing to ¼ inch and the dress Front to ½ inch.

Turn the facings to the wrong side. Edge baste and press lightly.

Lay out the dress Fronts wrong side up. Pin and baste the loose inner edges of the facings to the dress about 1 inch from the edge, so that the interfacing edge is accessible.

Baste the facing to the dress along the neck line.

Overcast the inner raw edge of the facing and stitch the interfacing to it with long running stitches. To do this, start the stitches about 10 inches above the hem line, work toward the shoulder seam and then across toward the neckline, so that the interfacing is firmly caught in position and so that it cannot roll or wrinkle during wear.

Darts and seams

Stitch the Front and Back darts and press them according to the fabric.

Pin, baste and stitch the shoulder and side seams. Finish the seam allowances and press seams open.

Turn under the seam allowance on the shoulderline of each Front facing and lightly hand sew it to the shoulder seam.

The collar

Following the collar instructions for the shirt in Dressmaking chapter 28, page 556, cut out the interfacings for the collar and collar band.

Then make the collar and band and stitch it to the dress.

The sleeves

Again following the shirt instructions in Dressmaking 28, p. 556, and 29, p. 576, cut out the cuff interfacing, make the cuffs and make the sleeve openings. Or, if you are working on a fine fabric, make the sleeve openings as shown for the tie-neck blouse in Dressmaking 41, page 814.

Pleat or gather the sleeve edge and attach the cuffs.

Make the buttonholes in the cuffs now, because the weight of the garments after the sleeves have been set in can be very irritating when making small buttonholes, even though the weight is supported.

Pin, baste and stitch the finished sleeves into the armholes. Trim and finish the armhole seams, then press them into the sleeves.

Hem, Front buttonholes and finishing

Pin and baste the hem, leaving the interfacing inside the hem. Fold in the ends of the facing over the hem and sew it down by hand (figure 3). Sew the hem, making very sure that the seam allowance on the Front edge is turned toward the facing in the hem (figure 2), otherwise you will have a thick ridge on the outside which will force the seam to roll outward when it is supposed to remain hidden just behind the edge of the wrap.

Check the button positions if you had to alter the length of the dress; then make the buttonholes by hand or machine. Sew on the buttons and give the dress a final pressing.

Make a tie belt to match from the remnants, following the instructions for tie belts in Dressmaking chapter 12, page 236.

B. Shirt dress with collar band finish

The neckline is the main feature of this version where the collar band has been

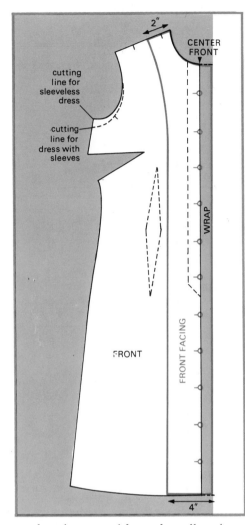

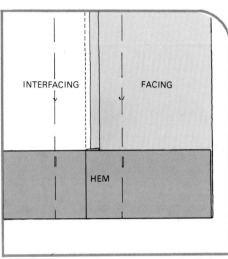

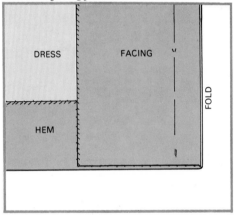

▲ 2. *Seam allowance turned toward facing in hem*
◀ 1. *Adapting the pattern for the shirt dress*
▼ 3. *Front facing folded and sewed over the hem*

used on its own without the collar. Apart from this detail, the dress is made with a button-down front and shirt sleeves as for version A.

The dress will look particularly attractive if the collar band and cuffs are made in a contrasting color to the rest of the dress.

The fabric

The fabric used should be firm as a soft fabric would roll and the shape of the collar band would be lost.

The pattern

You will need all the pattern pieces for version A except the shirt collar, number 10. Also adapt the pattern as for A.

Collar band. You can make the ends square or rounded. But remember that the square ends need two small buttons for fastening to stop the corner falling down.

Yardages

54in width. Without one way—sizes $32\frac{1}{2}$, 34 and 36, $2\frac{5}{8}$ yards; size 38, $2\frac{7}{8}$ yards; sizes 40 and 42, 3 yards.

54in width. With one way—size $32\frac{1}{2}$, $2\frac{5}{8}$ yards; size 34, $2\frac{3}{4}$ yards; size 36, $3\frac{1}{8}$ yards; sizes 38, 40 and 42, $3\frac{1}{4}$ yards.

36in width. Without one way—sizes $32\frac{1}{2}$

and 34, $3\frac{5}{8}$ yards; sizes 36 and 38, $3\frac{3}{4}$ yards; sizes 40 and 42, $4\frac{3}{8}$ yards.

36in width. With one way—sizes $32\frac{1}{2}$ and 34, $3\frac{5}{8}$ yards; sizes 36 and 38, $3\frac{3}{4}$ yards; sizes 40 and 42, $4\frac{1}{2}$ yards.

Notions

As for version A.

Cutting out, marking and fitting

Choose the correct layout for your style, size and fabric width from the layouts in this chapter.

Cut out, mark the details and fit the dress as for version A.

How to make the collar band

For this finish the collar band is worked in reverse to the one which you attach to a collar (see Dressmaking 28, p. 556).

Here you interface the outer, not inner, section of the collar band, and, with right sides facing, stitch the outer collar band to the neckline and then hand sew the inner section, or collar facing, to the seamline inside.

Making and finishing

Apart from the neck finish, the dress is made exactly as version A.

Layouts for the shirt dress: Version A

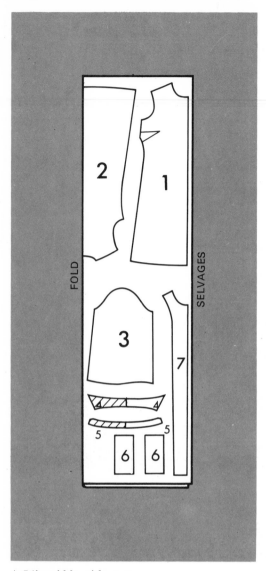

▲ *54in width, without one way,*
sizes 32½, 34, 36 & 38

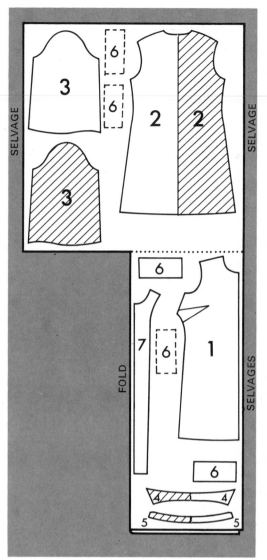

▲ *54in width, with and without one way,*
sizes 40 & 42

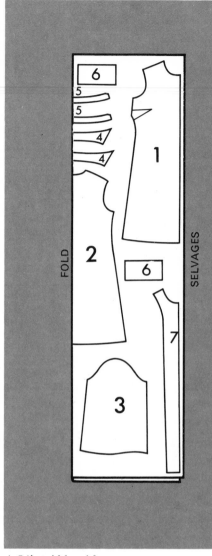

▲ *54in width, with one way,*
sizes 32½, 34, 36 & 38

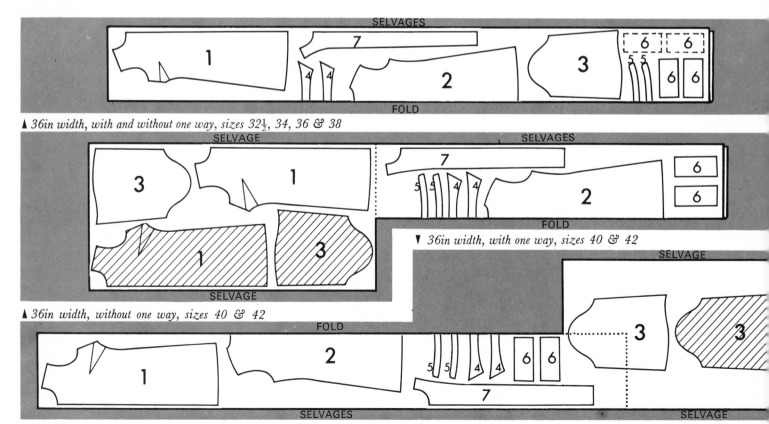

▲ *36in width, with and without one way, sizes 32½, 34, 36 & 38*

▲ *36in width, without one way, sizes 40 & 42*

▼ *36in width, with one way, sizes 40 & 42*

Version B

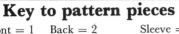

Key to pattern pieces

Front = 1   Back = 2   Sleeve = 3
Collar = 4   Collar band = 5   Cuff = 6
Front facing = 7

– – –   alternative for without one-way
/////   reverse pattern pieces

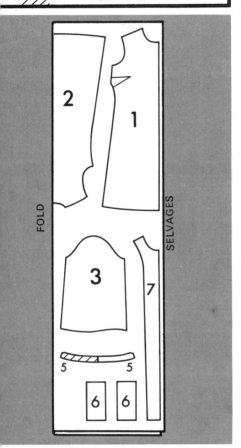

54in width, without one way,
sizes 32½, 34, 36 & 38

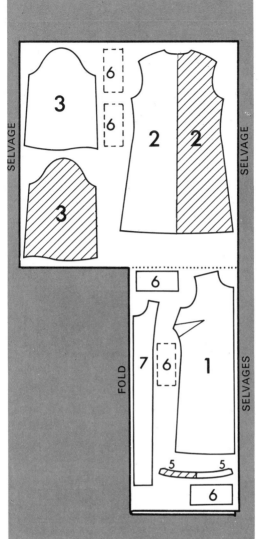

▲ 54in width, with and without one way,
sizes 40 & 42

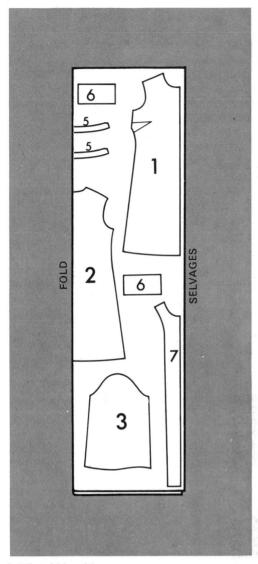

▲ 54in width, with one way,
sizes 32½, 34, 36 & 38

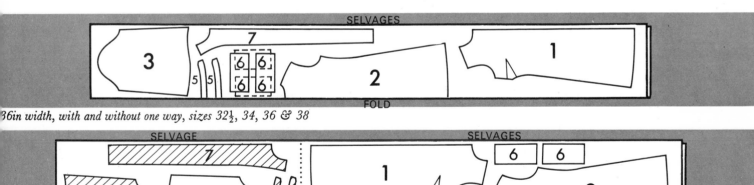

36in width, with and without one way, sizes 32½, 34, 36 & 38

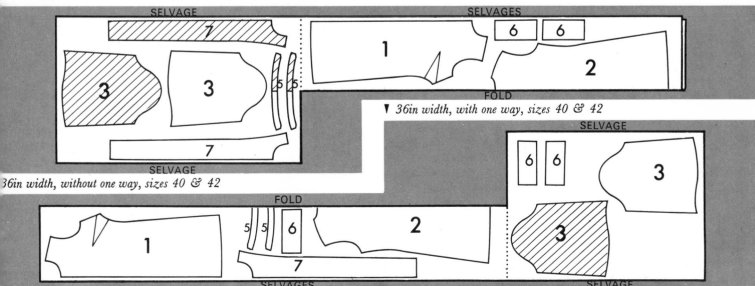

▼ 36in width, with one way, sizes 40 & 42

36in width, without one way, sizes 40 & 42

Furnishing Fashion Flair

Poppies and wheat

Scarlet red poppies and golden sprays of wheat are pretty embroidery motifs for household linens.

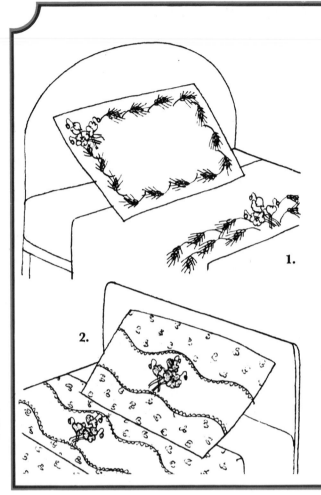

1. *Work bunches of poppies and stalks of wheat to make a pretty border on pillowcases and sheets.*

2. *Embroider the design on a plain contrasting fabric and apply it to the background material for a bold, modern style of decoration.*

3. *Work several bunches onto a shaped border to appliqué to a hand towel.*

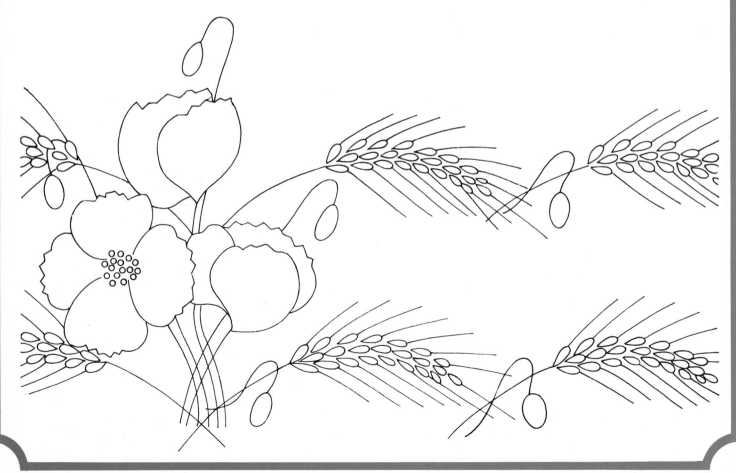

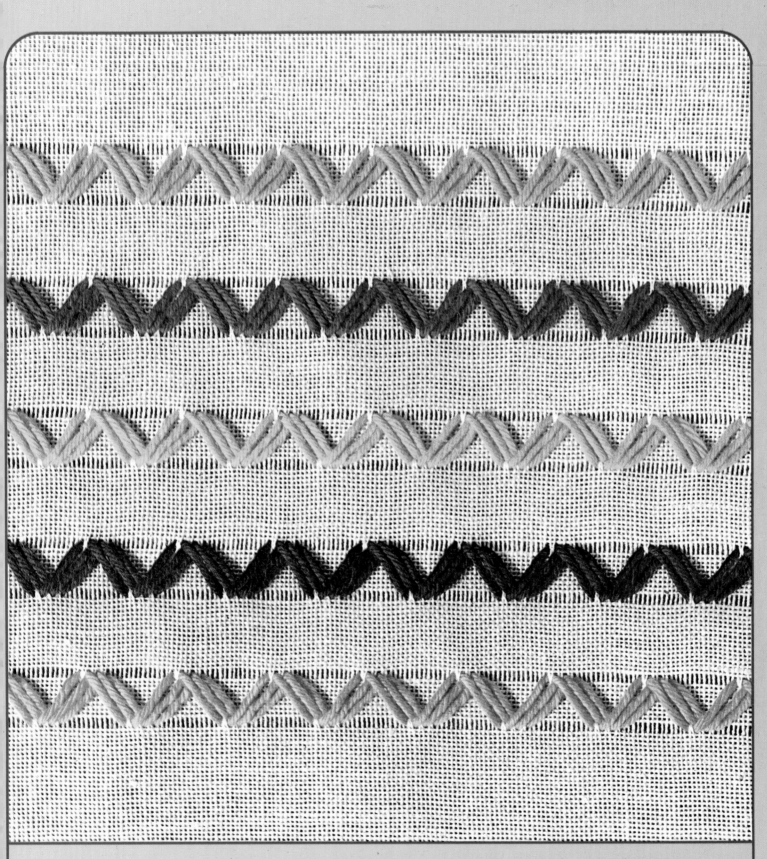

Pattern Library

Zigzags

This striking pattern darning design is worked in zigzags. First withdraw two threads from the fabric, leave nine, withdraw two more, leave sixteen and so on. Work on an even-weave fabric—linen, cotton or home furnishing fabric—with matte embroidery thread, 6-strand floss or pearl cotton. Pick up two threads on the bottom row of drawn threads, take the needle up to the next drawn thread row and eight across, pick up two threads. Continue to the end of the row, then work two more strands along the same row, each one picking up the next two threads along.

Mittens and gloves styled to fit

When gloves and mittens are worked on two needles, side and finger seams are necessary, but worked on sets of double-pointed needles they are smoothly seamless.

Choice of yarn

Select a yarn which is not too fine or too soft and will stand up to wear. Sports weight yarns are suitable and a yarn with a crepe finish would be an interesting texture choice. Needles should be finer than normal for the yarn you are using to give firm stitches which will not snag. A tight-fitting, weatherproof wrist ribbing is made by using needles one size smaller than used on the rest of the gloves or mittens. Remember that although the wrist must fit snugly, it must also be wide enough for the hand to be inserted easily.

▲ *Method of increasing for a thumb gusset, for both two and four needles*
▼ *Leaving the thumb gusset stitches on holder*

Calculating the number of stitches

As for any other garment, work a sample first so that you are satisfied that the pattern, the size of the needles and the type of yarn will together produce the surface you want. Measure the sample carefully to check how many stitches there are to the inch. The circumference of the hand just above the thumb division determines the number of inches you require. Multiply the number of inches needed by the number of stitches in one inch. For example, if your hand measures 7 inches around and the test sample of knitting produces 6 stitches to the inch, multiply 7 by 6, making 42, and cast on 42 stitches. This number of stitches appears to give a very loose wrist, but ribbing will draw in the extra width to make the wrist fit closely.

This number of stitches makes no allowance for the extra width below the thumb division, but this is usually worked as extra increasing in a triangular area between the wrist and thumb division. When sufficient stitches have been increased, they are slipped onto a stitch holder while extra stitches, to take their place, are cast on and then the remainder of the palm is worked.

Mittens on four needles

Size

To fit an average adult hand—the length is adjustable.

> **Gauge**
> $5\frac{1}{2}$ sts and $7\frac{1}{2}$ rows to 1in over stockinette stitch worked on No.5 needles.

Materials

Reynolds Classique—
2 (50 gram) balls
One set of No.5 double-pointed needles
(or Canadian No.8)
Stitch holder

Mittens

Begin at wrist edge. Cast on 40 sts. Work 2in K2, P2 rib.

Continue in st st. Working K every round, work 6 rounds.

Shape for thumb

1st round K2, K up thread before next st to inc, K next st and mark with colored thread as a guide to center thumb st, K up thread before next st to inc, K to end of round.

K 1 round.

3rd round K2, K up 1, K3, K up 1, K to end.

K 1 round.

Continue in this way, inc at either side of thumb gusset until 5 sts at either side have been inc.

K 1 round.

Next round K2, sl 11 sts for thumb onto holder, turn work and using 2-needle method cast on to left-hand needle 7 sts to replace thumb sts, turn and K to end of round.

Next round K1, sl 1 k-wise, K1, psso, K5, K2 tog, K to end.

K 1 round.

Next round K1, sl 1 k-wise, K1, psso, K3, K2 tog, K to end.

K 1 round.

Next round K1, sl 1 k-wise, K1, psso, K1, K2 tog, K to end.

Continue in st st until work measures 1in less than desired length to finger tip, or approximately $3\frac{1}{2}$in from thumb division.

Shape top

Dec 5 sts evenly on next round. K 1 round.
Rep last 2 rounds once.

Dec 5 sts evenly on next 5 rounds.

Break yarn, leaving an end long enough to thread through rem sts. Draw up and finish off.

Thumb

Attach yarn to thumb sts, K 6 sts from holder onto 1st needle, K rem 5 sts from holder onto 2nd needle and pick up and K7 sts along 7 cast-on sts.

Work in rounds of st st until 2in long, or 2 rounds less than desired length.

Next round *K1, K2 tog,
rep from * to end.
Last round *K2 tog, rep
from * to end.
Break off yarn and thread
through rem sts. Draw up and
finish off.
Make 2nd mitten in same
way. This reversible design
can be used for either hand.

Gloves on two needles

Size and gauge
As given for mittens.
Materials
Reynolds Classique—
2 (50 gram) balls
One pair No.5 needles
(or Canadian No.8)

Right hand

Begin at wrist. Cast on 40
sts. Work 1¼in K1, P1 rib.
1st patt row (RS) P.
2nd patt row *K1, P1, rep
from * to end.
These 2 rows form patt and
are rep throughout.
Continue in patt until work
measures 2½in from beg,
ending with a WS row.

Shape thumb

1st row P21 sts, inc in next
st by purling twice into same
st, P1 marking this as center
thumb st with colored
thread, inc in next st, P
rem 16 sts.
2nd row Patt to end.
3rd row P21 sts, inc 1, P3,
inc 1, P to end.
4th row As 2nd.
Keeping patt correct, continue
in this way, inc one st on
either side of center thumb st
on next and every other row
until 6 incs at either side
have been worked. (52 sts).
Next row Patt to last 22 sts,
turn and work on thumb sts
only.
Continue in patt across
thumb sts, inc one st at each
end of 1st row, until work
measures 2¼in, or desired
thumb length.
Last row *P2 tog, rep from
* to end.
Break yarn and thread
through rem sts. Draw up and
seam side of thumb.
With WS facing, attach yarn

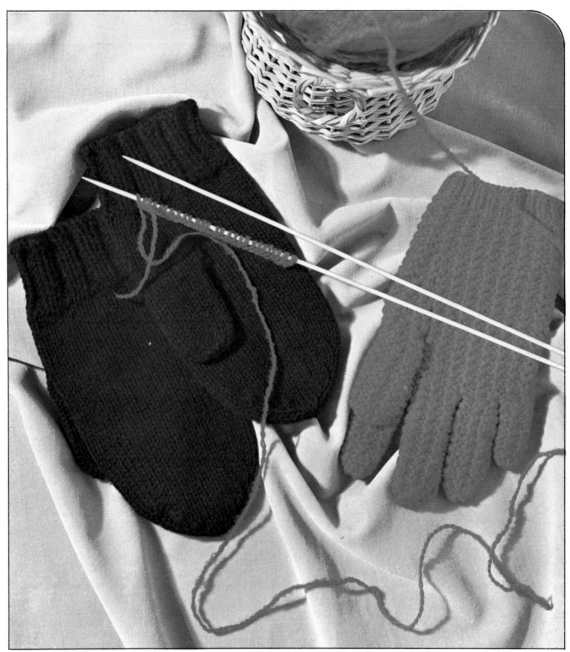

▲ *Simple and inexpensive accessories to make to coordinate with an outfit*

to 22 sts, work to end of row.
Next row Patt to thumb,
pick up and K4 sts from base
of thumb, patt to end of row.
(42 sts). Continue in patt until
work measures 5¼in from beg,
or desired length to division
for 1st finger ending with WS
row. Break yarn.
Attach yarn to 12 central
sts, leaving 15 sts on either
side on holders.

Work 1st finger
Continue in patt on 12 sts,
inc one st at each end of 1st
row for 2½in or desired
length, ending with a WS
row.

Last row *P2 tog, rep from
* to end.
Draw thread through rem
sts and seam finger.

Work 2nd finger
With RS facing, work 5 sts
from each holder and pick up
and K4 sts along lower edge of
1st finger.
Continue in patt on 14 sts,
inc one st at each end of 1st
row for 2¾in or desired
length, ending with a WS
row. Complete as for 1st
finger.

Work 3rd finger
Work as given for 2nd finger

until 2½in or desired length.
Complete as before.

Work little finger
Work 5 rem sts from each
holder and pick up and K4
sts from 3rd finger. Work as
before for 2¼in or desired
length. Complete as before.
Join little finger and side
seam.

Left hand

Work as given for right
hand, reversing all shaping.
1st shaping row will read:
P16, inc in next st, P1, inc
in next st, P to end.

Dress or button-down coat

This crocheted mini-cardigan in softest yarn can be worn as a button-down coat dress or as a tunic over pants. Make it in sparkling white with bands of lavender, light blue and navy as shown here or try French navy with scarlet and gray for the contrasting midriff panel.

Sizes
Directions are for 32in bust with 34in hips.
The figures in brackets [] refer to the 34, 36 and 38in bust sizes with 36, 38 and 40in hips, respectively.
Length to shoulder, 41[41½: 41½:42]in, adjustable.

Gauge
5dc and 2 rows to 1in worked on No.E crochet hook.

Materials
Reynolds Parfait (30gm balls)
9[11:12:13] balls of main color A
2[2:3:3] balls of contrast B
2 balls each of contrasts C and D
One No.D (3.00 mm) crochet hook
One No.E (3.50 mm) crochet hook
Nine buttons

Bodice

Using No.E crochet hook and B, ch136[146:156:166] and work bodice in one piece to underarm.
Base row Into 2nd ch from hook work 1sc, 1sc into each ch to end. Turn. 135[145: 155:165] sts.

Commence colored patt.
1st row Using B, ch2, skip first sc, 1sc into each sc to end. Turn.
2nd and 3rd rows As 1st.
4th row Using D, ch2, 1sc into first sc, *1sc into next sc, skip 1sc, 1sc into next sc, 2sc into each of next 2sc, rep from * to last 4sc, 1sc into next sc, skip 1sc, 1sc into next sc, 2sc into last sc. Turn. 162[174: 186:198] sts.
5th row Using D, ch2, 1sc into first sc, *1sc into next sc, skip 2sc, 1sc into next sc, 2sc into each of next 2sc, rep from * to last 4sc, skip 2sc, 1sc into next sc, 2sc into last sc. Turn.
6th and 7th rows Using C, as 5th. Break off C.
8th row Using D, ch2, skip first sc, *1dc into next sc, 1tr into each of next 2sc, 1dc into next sc, 1sc into each of next 2sc, rep from * to last 5sc, 1dc into next sc, 1tr into each of next 2sc, 1dc into next sc, 1sc into last sc. Turn.
9th row Using C, ch2, skip first st, *1sc into next st, 2sc into each of next 2 sts, 1sc into next st, skip 2 sts, rep from * ending skip 1 st. Turn.
10th row As 9th. Break off C.
11th and 12th rows Using D, as 9th and 10th. Break off D.
13th row Using B, ch2, skip first sc, 1sc into next sc, *skip next st, 1sc into each of next 5 sts, rep from * to last 4 sts, skip next st, 1sc into each of last 3 sts. Turn. 135[145:155: 165] sts.
Work rows 1-12 once more.
Change to No.D crochet hook and, using B, work 4 rows sc across all sts. 162[174:

186:198] sts. Break off B.
Change to No.E crochet hook and attach A.
1st row Ch3, skip first st, *1dc into next st, rep from * to end. Turn.
Rep this row until work measures 8½in from beg or desired length to underarm, ending with a WS row.

Divide for back and fronts
1st row Work in dc across 35[38:40:43] sts. Turn.
Complete right front on these sts.
Next row Ss across first st, work in dc to end. Turn.

Shape right front neck
Next row Ss across 9[9:10: 10] sts, work in dc to within 1 st of last st. Turn.
Next row Ss across first st, work in dc to within 1 st of last st. Turn. 22[25:26:29] sts.
Rep last row until 12[13:14: 15] sts rem.
Continue without shaping until armhole measures 6½[7: 7:7½]in from beg. Fasten off.
With RS of work facing, skip next 11[11:13:13] sts, attach yarn and work in dc across next 70[76:80:86] sts. Turn.
Complete back on these sts.
Next row Ss across first st, work in dc to within 1 st of last st. Turn.
Rep last row until 54[58:62: 66] sts rem.
Continue without shaping until back measures same as right front to shoulder. Fasten off.
With RS of work facing, skip next 11[11:13:13] sts, attach yarn to rem sts and work to end.
Complete left front on these sts.
Next row Work in dc to within 1 st of last st. Turn.

Shape left front neck
Next row Ss across first st, work in dc to last 9[9:10:10] sts. Turn.
Next row Ss across first st, work in dc to within 1 st of last st. Turn.
Rep last row until 12[13:14: 15] sts rem.
Complete to match right front.

Skirt

Using No.D crochet hook and A, with RS of work facing, attach yarn with ss to first st of left front.
1st row Ch3, 1dc into each of next 3[7:4:1] sts, (2dc into next st, 1dc into each of next 8[7:7:7] sts) 14[16:18:20] times, 2dc into next st, 1dc into each of next 4[8:5:2] sts. Turn. 150[162:174:186] sts.
2nd row Ch3, skip first st, * 1dc into next st, rep from * to end. Turn.
Change to No.E crochet hook. Work 3 rows dc.

Shape skirt
1st inc row Ch3, 1dc into each of next 11[12:13:14] sts, (2dc into next st, 1dc into each of next 24[26:28:30] sts) 5 times, 2dc into next st, 1dc into each of last 12[13:14:15] sts. Turn. 156[168:180:192] sts.
Work 3 rows dc.
2nd inc row Ch3, 1dc into each of next 11[12:13:14] sts, (2dc into next st, 1dc into each of next 25[27:29:31] sts) 5 times, 2dc into next st, 1dc into each of last 13[14:15:16] sts. Turn. 162[174:186:198] sts.
Work 3 rows dc.
3rd inc row Ch3, 1dc into each of next 12[13:14:15] sts, (2dc into next st, 1dc into each of next 26[28:30:32] sts) 5 times, 2dc into next st, 1dc into each of last 13[14:15:16] sts. Turn. 168[180:192:204] sts.
Work 5 rows dc.
4th inc row Ch3, 1dc into each of next 12[13:14:15] sts, (2dc into next st, 1dc into each of next 27[29:31:33] sts) 5 times, 2dc into next st, 1dc into each of last 14[15:16:17] sts. Turn. 174[186:198:210] sts.
Work 5 rows dc.
5th inc row Ch3, 1dc into each of next 13[14:15:16] sts, (2dc into next st, 1dc into each of next 28[30:32:34] sts) 5 times, 2dc into next st, 1dc into each of last 14[15:16:17] sts. Turn. 180[192:204:216] sts.
Work 7 rows dc.
6th inc row Ch3, 1dc into each of next 13[14:15:16] sts, (2dc into next st, 1dc into each of next 29[31:33:35] sts) 5 times, 2dc into next st, 1dc into

each of last 15[16:17:18] sts.
Turn. 186[198:210:222] sts.
Work 7 rows dc.

7th inc row Ch3, 1dc into
each of next 14[15:16:17] sts,
(2dc into next st, 1dc into each
of next 30[32:34:36] sts) 5
times, 2dc into next st, 1dc into
each of last 15[16:17:18] sts.
Turn. 192[204:216:228] sts.
Work 7 rows dc.

8th inc row Ch3, 1dc into
each of next 14[15:16:17] sts,
(2dc into next st, 1dc into each
of next 31[33:35:37] sts) 5
times, 2dc into next st, 1dc into
each of last 16[17:18:19] sts.
Turn. 198[210:222:234] sts.
Work 9 rows dc.

9th inc row Ch3, 1dc into
each of next 15[16:17:18] sts,
(2dc into next st, 1dc into each
of next 32[34:36:38] sts) 5
times, 2dc into next st, 1dc
into each of last 16[17:18:19]
sts. Turn. 204[216:228:240]
sts.

Continue without shaping
until work measures 40½[41:
41:41½]in from top of shoulder,
or desired length less ½in.
Fasten off.

Finishing

Press on WS under a damp
cloth using a warm iron. Join
shoulder seams.
Armbands Using No.D
crochet hook and B, with RS
facing, work 1 row sc around
armhole. Turn. Work 2 more
rows sc. Fasten off.
Front borders Using No.
D crochet hook and B, with
RS facing, work in sc up
right front edge, around neck,
down left front and around
lower edge, working 3sc into
each corner st. Turn.
Next row (buttonhole row)
Work in sc, making 9
buttonholes on right front
edge, the 1st to come just
below neck shaping and rem
8, 2½in apart, by working ch3
and skipping 3sc, and working
3sc into each corner st. Turn.
Next row Work in sc to end,
working 3sc into each ch3
buttonhole on previous row.
Fasten off.
Join armbands. Press borders.
Sew on buttons to correspond
with buttonholes.

845

Shaping corners in filet

▲ 1. *Decreasing a space at the end of a row*

Shaping and making corners in filet crochet is not difficult but the continuity of the pattern must be kept accurate. Here are some useful hints for increasing and decreasing on spaces and blocks and a pretty filet crochet edging to sample.

Decreasing a space at the end of a row

At the end of the row where shaping is required, do not work last space but turn work, ch5 and work 1dc into 2nd dc of row below (figure **1**).

Decreasing a space at the beginning of a row

Work last space of previous row, turn. On next row, ch1, work 1ss into each of the next 2 ch sts, 1ss into next dc, ch5, skip 2ch, 1dc into next dc, *ch2, skip 2ch, 1dc into next dc, rep from * to end (figure **2**).

Increasing a space at the beginning of a row

Complete the row before shaping is required, turn work. On next row, ch7 (2 for base, 3 for side and 2 for top of space), work 1dc into last dc of previous row, *ch2, skip 2ch, 1dc into next dc, rep from * to end (figure **3**).

Decreasing a block at the end of a row

Work in pattern to the last 4dc, work 1dc, turn.
Next row. Ch3 if next row commences with a block, 3dc and then continue in pattern. Begin with ch5 if next row commences with a space, skip 2ch or 2dc, depending on whether you are working over a space or a block, 1dc into next dc, continue in pattern.

Increasing a block at the beginning of a row

Complete to the end of the row before shaping is required, turn work and ch5. Work 1dc into 4th ch from hook and 1dc into 5th ch from hook, then continue working in pattern to end.

Filet crochet edging

Practice reading from a chart to work this edging, remembering that each open square represents a space and each dot a block of doubles. Ch24 and to start 1st row work (1 block, 1 space) 4 times, reading chart from single asterisk and working in rows from right to left, then left to right. When 18th row of chart has been worked, start shaping first side of corner by mitering the edge as follows:
1st row. Ch1, skip 1dc, ss over next 3dc, ch5, skip 2ch, (1 block, 1 space) twice, 1 block. Turn.
2nd row. Ch3, 1 block, 2 spaces, 1 block, 1 space. Turn.
3rd row. Ch1, 2ss into 2ch, 1ss into 1dc, ch5, skip 2ch, 1 block, 1 space, 1 block, Turn.
4th row. Ch3, 1 block, 2 spaces. Turn.
5th row. Ch1, 2ss into 2ch, 1ss into 1dc, ch5, skip 2ch, 1 block. Turn.
6th row. Ch3, 1 block.

▲ 2. *Decreasing a space at the beginning of a row*
▼ 3. *Increasing a space at the beginning of a row*

7th row. (1st row of turning corner) Ch3, 2dc into side of previous block, ss to corner ch of 5ch.
8th row. Ch2, 1dc into corner after 3ss, turn work, 1 block. Turn.
9th row. Ch3, 1 block, 1 space, 1 block, (2dc and ss to corner).
10th row. Ch3, 2dc into space, ss to corner, ch1, turn work then work 3ss along next 2dc and top of ch, 2 spaces, 1 block. Turn.
11th row. Ch3, (1 block, 1 space) twice, 1 block, (2dc into space, ss into corner ch).
12th row. Ch2, 1dc into turning ch of block, turn work, 1 space, 2 blocks, 1 space, 1 block. Turn.
13th row. Ch3, 1 block, 1 space, 3 blocks, 1 space, 1 block in side of dc block.
Now continue as given on chart, working from double asterisk.

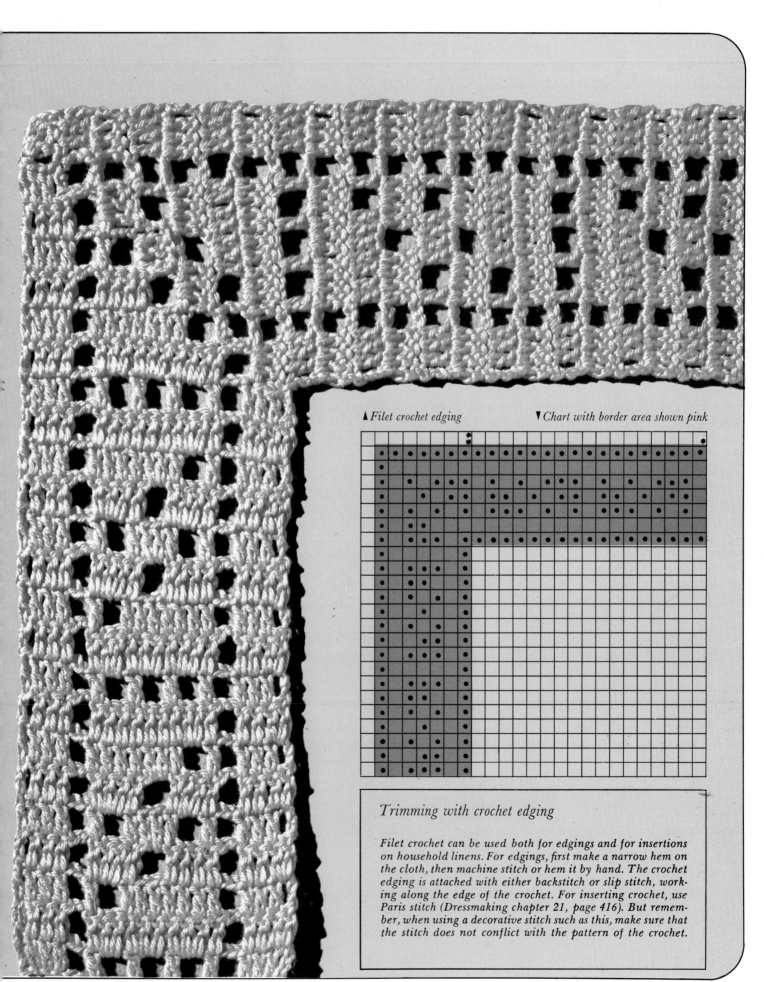

▲ *Filet crochet edging* ▼ *Chart with border area shown pink*

Trimming with crochet edging

Filet crochet can be used both for edgings and for insertions on household linens. For edgings, first make a narrow hem on the cloth, then machine stitch or hem it by hand. The crochet edging is attached with either backstitch or slip stitch, working along the edge of the crochet. For inserting crochet, use Paris stitch (Dressmaking chapter 21, page 416). But remember, when using a decorative stitch such as this, make sure that the stitch does not conflict with the pattern of the crochet.

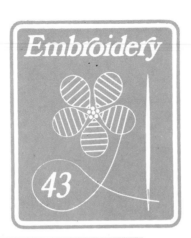

Introduction to blackwork

Stitch Library

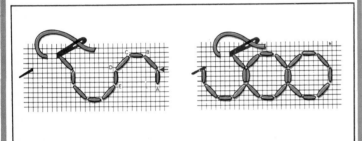

Ringed backstitch
Alternate halves of the circles are worked in backstitch and completed on the return journey. This stitch can be used as a filling or border stitch.

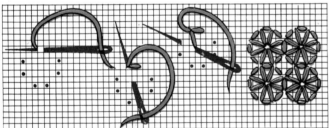

Eyelet filling stitch
A pretty filling stitch of eyelets with a backstitch worked over two threads of fabric between the spokes of the stitch.

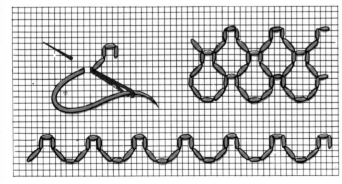

Festoon
This filling stitch is worked in backstitch. It can also be used in horizontal lines.

Blackwork embroidery was probably of African origin and introduced to Spain by the Moors. Although blackwork was not entirely unknown in England, Henry VIII's Spanish wife Katharine of Aragon increased its popularity, and throughout Tudor and Elizabethan times the embroidery was used extensively on clothes and gradually came to be used on household linens such as bed hangings.

The delightful panel of fishes in this chapter has been specially designed for Creative Hands as a modern interpretation of blackwork, and though it may at first sight appear complicated the design can be easily copied from the picture. Each fish can be used as a separate motif.

In simple terms, blackwork is a monochrome method of embroidery. It relies for effect on the relationships of tone values and consists of a variety of light fillings in well-planned shapes with neatly defined outlines. Traditionally worked in black on white with additional touches of gold and silver threads, the dramatic tone contrast has always been the main attraction of this method.

In modern embroidery design, however, color has been introduced. The choice of color or colors needs considerable care and the stronger the contrast the more dramatic the effect. Experiment with color contrasts and combinations of colors such as white embroidery on black, red on pink, brown on cream or beige, until you achieve the desired effect and your own individual style.

Blackwork can be used to great effect on all types of clothing such as blouses, dresses and skirts, or on household linens such as runners, tablecloths, place mats, curtains, pillows and wall panels. Stitches in blackwork are worked over counted threads of evenweave fabric and as a result designs tend to be angular. However, areas of filling can be tapered off to produce more rounded or pointed shapes which do not have to be enclosed in an outline stitch. Alternatively, flowing lines of stitching can be incorporated as an integral part of a design to give a freer feeling. Certain pattern lines and shapes can be strengthened by using a thicker yarn or by working over fewer threads of fabric, whereas lighter areas are created by working with finer yarn or by working over more threads of fabric.

Fabrics
Suitable fabrics include embroidery linen, or synthetic dress or home furnishing fabrics with a precise even weave of between thirteen to thirty-nine threads to the inch, provided the threads are clear enough to count.

Yarns
Generally speaking, the thickness of the yarns should correspond to the threads of the fabric, but this can vary depending on the final effect required.

Six-strand floss, pearl cotton, sewing thread, machine embroidery thread, matte embroidery cotton and various kinds of metal threads (see Embroidery chapters 37, page 728, and 38, page 748) can all be used in blackwork. To keep the effect precise, it is best to use single thread in the needle, but for a softer effect use two or three strands of six-strand floss.

Stitches
Blackwork outlines can be worked in a variety of stitches such as outline stitch, backstitch, whipped backstitch, coral stitch and couching.

Filling stitches, which are used to form the patterns, are based on straight stitches—running stitch, backstitch and double running or Holbein stitch. Cross-stitch and its variations are also used as filling stitches, and darning, which is one of the simplest forms of embroidery, makes an interesting filling

Double running stitch (Holbein stitch). This stitch is worked in two stages by working running stitch over the counted threads and then a second row filling the spaces left by the first.

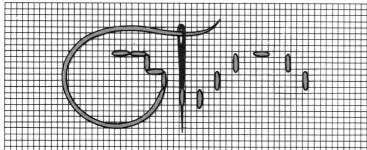

▲ *The two stages of working double running stitch*

Eye stitch. Worked with eight stitches of equal length radiating from a central point.

Coral stitch. Working from right to left, bring thread up through the fabric and hold with the thumb of the left hand. Take a small stitch at right angles to the thread, going under and over it. Pull up to form a small knot.

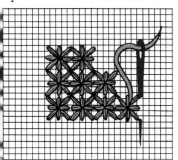

▲ *Method of working eye stitch*   ▲ *Method of working coral stitch*

Page 849

Transferring designs
Use the trace and baste method for transferring designs, described in Embroidery chapter 4, page 68.

Using a frame
It is advisable to use a frame for this type of embroidery. A hoop is suitable for small pieces of work and a square frame for larger pieces.

A blackwork panel of fishes for you to copy shown life-size ►
▼ One of the fishes in the panel enlarged to show detail

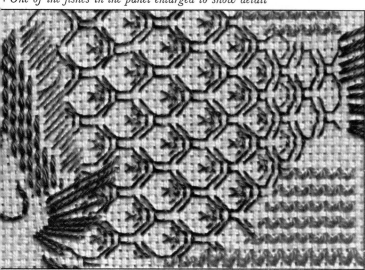

Director's chair flower panels

Directors' style chairs are easy to cover and look marvelous in brilliant embroidery. The stylized flower design in this chapter is simple to copy and looks best in a modern setting.

The modern canvas chair can vary in styling detail. In this chapter you will find two basic methods of making covers and one or the other will adapt to most variations.

Pop-on cover (photographs)

This type of cover simply fits over the original back and seat sections and is easily removed for cleaning purposes.

Materials you will need
- ☐ Canvas with 10 double threads to the inch
- ☐ Tapestry yarns
- ☐ Sateen lining
- ☐ Snap fastener tape for attaching cover
- ☐ Plastic foam 1in thick (optional)

▼ *Detail of the chair design on the opposite page*

To make a pattern

Pin a sheet of strong paper over and around the fabric back and another over the seat of the chair. With a pencil, mark the edges of the shape onto the paper. Remove the paper and even up the shape before cutting out. Once the pieces are cut out, check them against the back and seat to make sure that they fit well.

Pin the pieces onto canvas, following the grain lines of the canvas. Mark the outline onto the canvas with a felt-tipped pen, leaving sufficient canvas all around for seam allowances and blocking.

Completing the embroidery

Plan the flower design as described in Needlepoint 19, p. 752, using the chart on the following pages. Work the design in tent stitch or cross-stitch over two sets of double threads each way. When it is completed, block and trim the canvas as described in Needlepoint 5, p. 112, leaving ⅝ inch turnings at the edges.

Padding

For additional comfort, pad between the canvas and the lining with one-inch thick plastic foam.

To make the cover

Cut the lining to the exact size of the stitched and trimmed canvas.

Turn seam allowances to the back and baste. Turn all canvas raw edges to the back of the work and catch in place. Line the shapes with sateen lining. Stitch lengths of snap fastener tape to each end of the needlepoint back and seat sections and then onto the corresponding areas on the actual chair.

Slip cover (drawings)

This type of cover has tube openings at each side of the back section to slip over the back supports, and also at each side of the seat section to slide on rods which are held in place by the structure of the chair. This cover replaces the original back and seat covers on the chair.

Materials you will need
- ☐ Canvas with 10 double threads to the inch
- ☐ Tapestry yarns
- ☐ Dull-finish cotton such as sailcloth for lining back
- ☐ Canvas or burlap (optional) for lining seat

To make the cover

Because the original sections are removed from the chair first, they can be used as a pattern guide. Cut out the pattern and work the embroidery as for the pop-on cover.

Line the back section as for the pop-on cover with sailcloth. The seat of the chair must be reinforced either by backing it with strong canvas or burlap or by using the original seat section.

Once the backing has been stitched to the needlepoint, turn under the ends as on the original sections and sew. Slide into place on the chair frame.

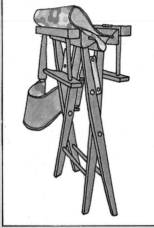

▲ *The director's chair folded*
▼ *The back and seat sections*

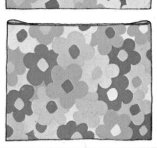

▲ *Slip-on back and seat of chair*
▼ *The director's chair complete*

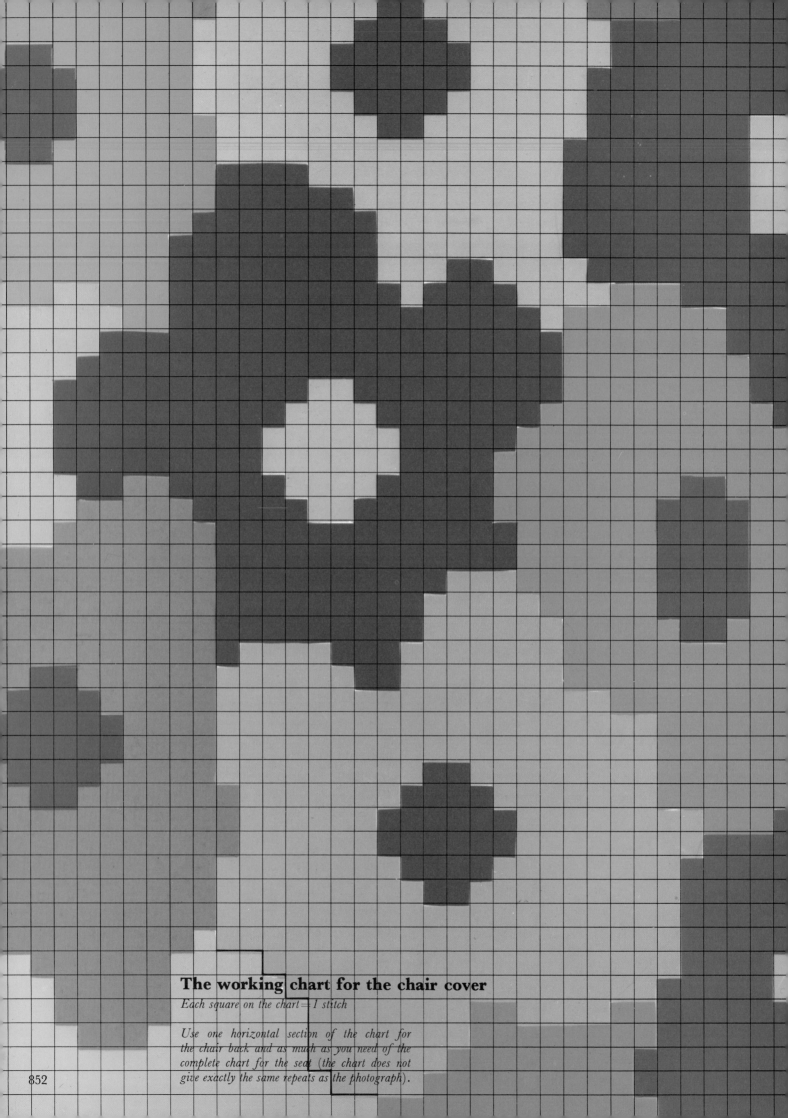

The working chart for the chair cover

Each square on the chart = 1 stitch

Use one horizontal section of the chart for the chair back and as much as you need of the complete chart for the seat (the chart does not give exactly the same repeats as the photograph).

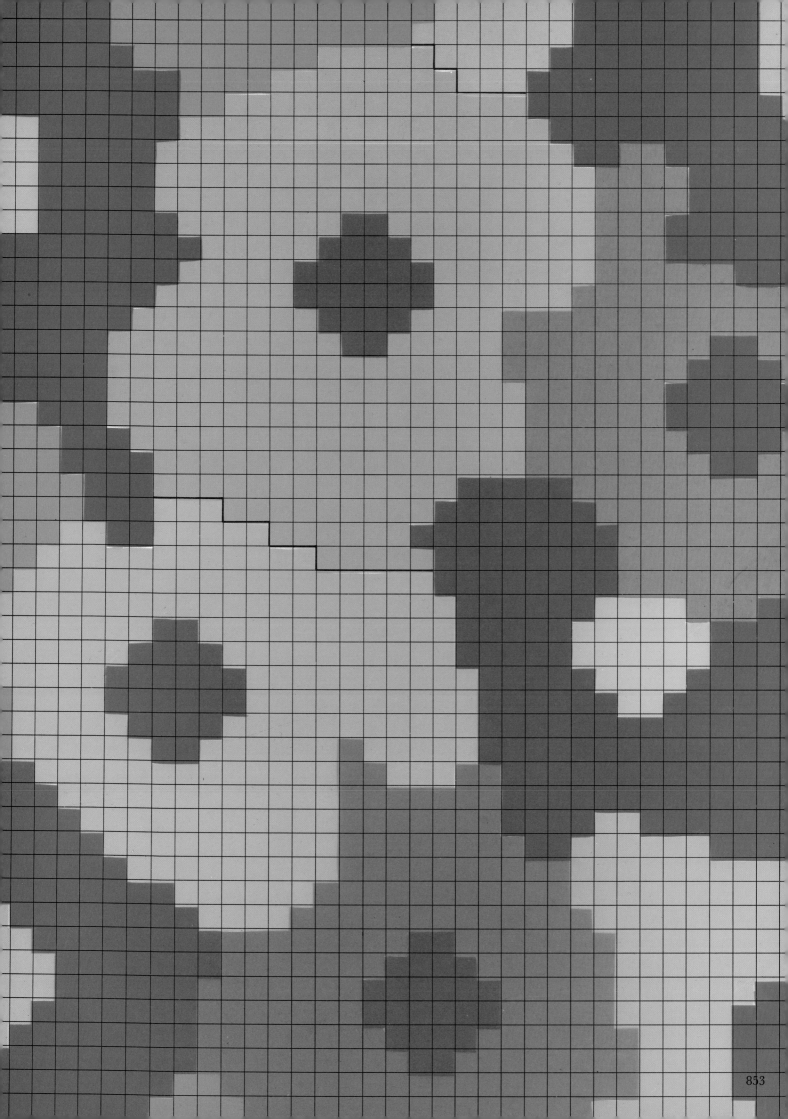

853

Needlemade lace the Danish way

Needle-made lace 4

Danish lace is a form of needle-made lace. As the name indicates, it originated in Denmark where it was used to decorate household linen. The peasant women also used it to make their coarse linen clothing more attractive.

It consists of various motifs worked directly onto the edges of the fabric, or of inserts made by cutting out shapes from the material and filling the cutout shapes with decorative stitches. These are mostly buttonhole stitch and variations of buttonhole stitch, built up into the design shapes. Traditional Danish embroidery was usually worked on hand-woven linen in white. Drawn threadwork and these lace fillings were introduced to give an attractive variation. White work still has a classic beauty but the use of color gives a more modern appeal to the designs.

When working Danish lace, always make sure that the thread is a suitable thickness for the fabric to be embroidered. When working insets, always pin the material to a piece of cardboard and baste so that the cutout shape does not become distorted during working.

Buttonhole stitch
In Danish lace the filling stitches are worked on a foundation of buttonhole stitch. Fold the edge of the fabric over once and, working from left to right, insert the needle downward, bringing it out below the folded edge. Pull the thread through until a loop is formed and, holding the thread to the right, thread the needle through the loop from top to bottom. Finish the stitch by firmly pulling the thread upward.

Twisted buttonhole stitch
Working from right to left, insert the needle into the fabric and pull the needle through to form a fairly loose loop. Thread the needle through the loop from bottom to top, left to right, and pull firmly upward.

Once the row is completed, the stitch can be strengthened by overcasting the top horizontal bars.

Buttonhole motif with picot
Work a base row of evenly spaced buttonhole stitches. Slot the thread back through the fabric to make two padding stitches by making a loop over several buttonhole stitches, thread the needle back through the fabric and make another loop in the same way. Slot the needle back through the fabric again, taking the thread back to the beginning of the padding loops. The number of stitches worked over depends on the size of loop required.

Work buttonhole stitch along the padding loops until the point where the picot is to be positioned.

Make a buttonhole stitch leaving it fairly loose. Insert the needle from right to left through the back of the knot of the previous buttonhole stitch. Work a buttonhole stitch on the picot and then thread the needle through the picot from left to right, back to front.

Continue in buttonhole stitch along the remaining part of the padding loop.

Buttonhole loops can be worked at spaced intervals or side by side along an edge.

Circular insert
Trace a circle onto the material and baste the fabric onto a piece of cardboard. Using a pair of sharp, finely pointed scissors, cut out the circle $\frac{1}{4}$ inch from the outline.

Snip the edge and then fold the material along the traced line to the back of the work, and make a buttonhole stitch edging with one stitch every tenth of an inch. Next, work one row of twisted buttonhole stitch, making one stitch for every two in the previous

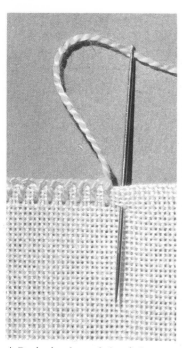

▲ *Beginning buttonhole stitch*

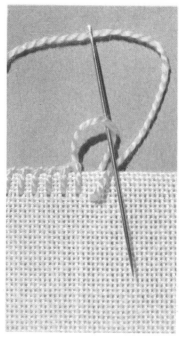

▲ *Knotting the buttonhole loop*

▼ *Twisted buttonhole stitch, the needle inserted from front of fabric*

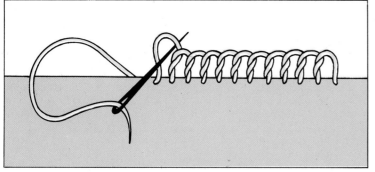

▼ *Overcasting the top bar of each twisted buttonhole stitch*

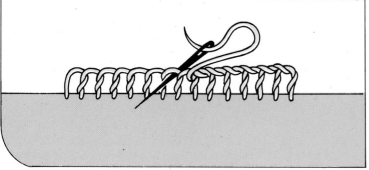

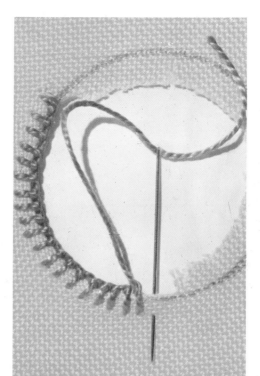

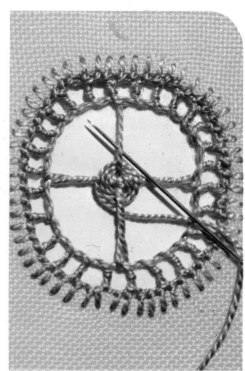

▲ *Forming a picot on the buttonhole loop motif*
▼ *Working a buttonhole stitch on the picot*

▲ *Working buttonhole stitch foundation on insert*
▼ *A pretty edging lace formed from buttonhole stitch loops*

▲ *The final stage of a decorative insert*

row. Overcast the top horizontal bars of the twisted buttonhole stitches a quarter of the way around the circle. Without cutting the thread, take it directly across the circle, slipping the needle up through the buttonhole loop and then overcast back across the thread.

Continue around the circle, overcasting the top horizontal bars of the twisted buttonhole stitches until the starting point is reached. Take the thread directly across the circle, slipping the needle up through the buttonhole loop and then work back across the thread as before to the center point of the cross. Weave around the cross for three or four rounds and then overcast back along the remaining spoke. Darn the thread through to the back of the fabric and finish off neatly.

Edging lace

1st row. Work buttonhole stitch along the fabric edge.

2nd row. Work one twisted buttonhole stitch for every three stitches in the previous row.

3rd row. Work three buttonhole stitches into each of the first two spaces. To form a bar take the thread over, skipping four spaces, and attach it to the previous row. Work back across this bar with buttonhole stitch and then continue working three buttonhole stitches into each of the spaces below. Repeat to the end of the row.

4th row. Work twisted buttonhole stitch to form five spaces on the bar and two spaces between the bars.

5th row. Cover the previous row with buttonhole stitch, working a picot on the center space of each scallop.

Shirt dress conversion

The shirt dress story, which began in chapter 42, page 834, with instructions for version A and B, continues here with this glamorous evening shirt dress, version C.

This style is flattering to all age groups and it is easy and comfortable to wear. It can be dressed up for really formal occasions or left plain and elegant to make the perfect dinner gown. It travels well, too. Made in a light, printed silk you have something ideal for holiday wear—a gown in which you can feel both well-dressed and relaxed. This chapter includes the instructions for making this dress with the layouts on pages 858 and 859. Also included are layouts for version D, the shirt dress with full, bishop sleeves. The instructions for adapting the pattern and making this sleeve follow in the concluding chapter of this ingenious tale!

C. The evening shirt dress

Suitable fabrics

The fabric used will dictate the mood of this shirt dress. While all those mentioned in Dressmaking chapter 42 are suitable, this style lends itself particularly well to evening wear fabrics.

Made sleeveless, in heavy brocade, it becomes an elegant gown for formal occasions, but made in a lovely printed hand-woven Indian silk, like the one in the photograph, it becomes the type of garment which can be worn on many occasions. A characteristic of these silks is their slightly creased appearance which complements the casual look of the dress.

The pattern

You will need the following pattern pieces from the Creative Hands Pattern Pack given in Volume 22.

From the dress pattern sheet, the Front, Back and tab pattern pieces, numbers 1, 2 and 3.

From the accessory pattern sheet, the shirt collar and collar band pattern pieces, numbers 10 and 11.

The right Front pattern. For this dress you need a right Front pattern piece and one for the left Front.

First copy the Front pattern using a sheet of paper which is long enough to include the extra length needed for the evening dress. Place the Center Front of the pattern along one edge of the paper as shown (figure 1) and draw around the pattern.

Copy the stitching line for the tab.

Measure the extra length you need for the evening dress. Starting at the side seam, measure off this amount from the hem edge with a yardstick. Continue doing this along the full width of the hem, so that you retain the original shape of the hem, and draw in the new lines as shown.

Remove the original pattern and cut out the new one along the solid line in figure 1.

The left Front pattern. In Dressmaking chapter 10, page 196, it was mentioned that a conventional wrap would be cut later, and now is the time to do this.

Place the original Front pattern on a large sheet of paper as before, but reversing it and with the Center Front of the pattern 1 inch from the straight edge (figure 2).

Draw around the shape of the pattern and extend the length as for the right Front.

Draw in the tab stitching line and connect the pointed end to the straight edge of the paper, drawing a straight line across. Cut out the new pattern along the solid cutting line. The 1 inch extension above the pointed end of the tab stitching line is the wrap for the front opening.

The Back pattern. Copy the Back pattern piece on a sheet of paper long enough to include the extra length needed for the

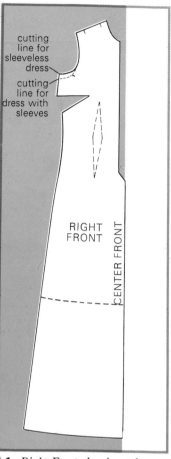

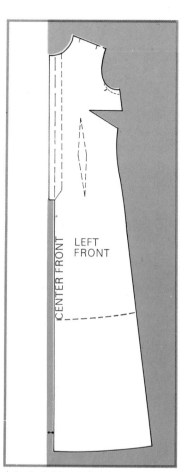

cutting line for sleeveless dress

cutting line for dress with sleeves

RIGHT FRONT

CENTER FRONT

LEFT FRONT

CENTER FRONT

CENTER FRONT

INTERFACING

LEFT FRONT wrong side

▲ **1.** *Right Front showing tab stitching line and length extended*

▼ **3.** *Wrap and tab facing*

▲ **2.** *Left Front showing wrap extension and length extended*

▼ **4.** *Interfacing inside of wrap*

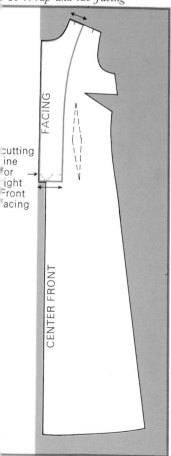

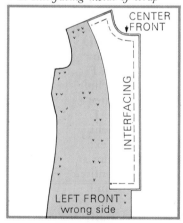

FACING

cutting line for right front facing

CENTER FRONT

CENTER FRONT

▼ **5.** *Topstitching collar and band*

evening dress, then draw in the new hemline as for the Front pattern pieces.

Facing patterns. To make the facing patterns for the tab and wrap, pin the Center Front of the left pattern piece along the straight edge of a sheet of paper. Draw around the shape of the neck and shoulderlines and mark the lower end of the wrap. Remove the pattern, measure out the width of the facing and complete as shown (figure **3**). Cut out the facing pattern. This outline is for the wrap facing.

For the tab facing outline, pin the tab pattern piece to the front edge of the facing pattern and draw the shape of the pointed end, extending it straight to the inner edge as shown (see dotted line, figure **3**). Use this line when cutting the facing for the tab, but do not cut out along this line yet.

Yardages

48in width. Without one way—size $32\frac{1}{2}$, $2\frac{7}{8}$ yards; size 34, 3 yards; size 36, $3\frac{1}{8}$ yards; size 38, $3\frac{3}{8}$ yards; size 40, $3\frac{5}{8}$ yards; size 42, $3\frac{3}{4}$ yards.

48in width. With one way — sizes $32\frac{1}{2}$, 34 and 36, $3\frac{5}{8}$ yards; sizes 38, 40 and 42, $3\frac{7}{8}$ yards.

36in width. Without one way — sizes $32\frac{1}{2}$ and 34, 4 yards; size 36, $4\frac{1}{4}$ yards; sizes 38 and 40, $4\frac{1}{2}$ yards; size 42, $4\frac{3}{4}$ yards.

36in width. With one way—sizes $32\frac{1}{2}$ and 34, 4 yards; size 36, $4\frac{1}{2}$ yards; size 38, $4\frac{5}{8}$ yards; size 40, $4\frac{3}{4}$ yards; size 42, $4\frac{7}{8}$ yards.

Notions

You will need:

☐ 6 small buttons
☐ Matching thread
☐ Interfacing, the length of the front facing plus $1\frac{1}{2}$ inches for seam allowance, or interlining (see below)

Interlinings and interfacings

If you want to line this dress, use a fully mounted interlining chosen to complement the fabric of the dress, such as a Japanese silk lining for pure silks and fine rayon taffeta for brocades. The interlining is cut out the same way as the dress fabric, using the layout and yardage for the 36in width without one way. It is then basted to the fabric and used as one. This way you will not need an interfacing. If you decide not to interline the dress, you will need interfacing for the tab, wrap, collar and collar band. See Dressmaking chapter 42, page 834, for suitable interfacings.

Cutting and marking

To cut out the evening shirt dress you will need a very large area to work on since the full length of the dress is cut in one.

Choose the correct layout for your style, size and fabric width from the layouts, pages 858 and 859. Lay out the fabric carefully, pinning the selvages and folds to make sure that they cannot move.

The pattern has no seam or hem allowances, so mark $\frac{3}{4}$ inch for seams and $2\frac{1}{2}$ inches for hems all around.

Cut both tab and wrap facings together, using the wrap facing pattern piece. The tab facing will be trimmed to shape later.

Note that the shirt collar and collar band are cut on the same grain of the fabric.

Cut two bias strips $1\frac{1}{2}$ inches wide for the armhole facings, joining the strips to make the desired length if necessary.

Trim the wrap facing pattern piece along the dotted line for the tab facing, then trim one of the facings for the tab, similarly—don't forget to add the seam allowance.

Mounting the fabric

If you are mounting the dress, cut out the interlining as for the dress and baste it to the wrong side of each dress piece.

Interfacing

If you are not lining the dress, cut one collar, one collar band, one tab and one wrap facing piece from interfacing, adding seam allowance on all edges except the inner edge of the wrap facing.

Baste the corresponding interfacing pieces to the wrong side of the top collar and outer collar band sections, and the tab. Also baste the wrap interfacing to the inside of the wrap (see figure **4** on previous page) on the left Front.

Stitching the Front fastening

Since it is not possible to pin the Center Front at the top of the dress for fitting, it is best to make the Front fastening detail before you try and fit the dress. It is possible to do so as there will be no alteration to this particular area.

Make the tab as you did for the basic dress in Dressmaking chapters 10, p. 196, and 11, p. 216, using the front facing with the shaped end to face the tab. Do not stitch the tab and facing together along the neck edge—this remains open to take the collar band. To avoid thick seam edges on the tab if you are using it, trim the seam allowance of the interfacing to $\frac{1}{8}$ inch.

Stitch the Center Front of the dress from the pointed end of the tab stitching line to the hem. Finish the seam and press open. Stitch on the tab and finish the pointed end inside as for the basic dress, but do not fold, and sew the inner facing edge to the stitching line.

Topstitch the tab $\frac{1}{4}$ inch from the edges.

Face the left Front of the dress with the straight ended facing. Do not stitch along the neck edge. It is not necessary to stitch across the lower end of the wrap; this often creates an unwanted thickness and it is best to leave it open.

Trim the interfacing seam allowance to $\frac{1}{8}$ inch if you are using it. Finish the wrap end inside as for the basic dress, but do not fold, and sew the wrap facing down on the inner edge.

If you have used interfacing on the wrap, attach the inner edges to the facing with loose catch stitches.

Overcast the inner edges to finish off.

Fitting and finishing the dress

Baste and fit the evening dress making any necessary adjustments. Stitch the darts and seams, and finish the armhole and hem edges as for the basic dress, Dressmaking ch. 10, pg. 196, and 11, pg. 216. Interface collar and band (if necessary), stitch together, then attach to dress as instructed in Dressmaking chapter 28, pg. 556. Topstitch collar and band to match the tab (figure **5** on previous page). Make buttonholes and sew on buttons to finish.

Finishes with mounted interlinings

After stitching and pressing the seams open, carefully trim the seam allowance and overcast by hand to finish. Avoid machine finishes in any way since they tend to curl the two layers of fabric creating a thick and hard seam edge; this in turn makes an impression through the fabric, often showing up noticeably on the outside of the dress.

Facings should be lightly caught to seamlines and not be firmly sewn in place. So work under the facing edge and hand sew loosely. To prevent the interlining from folding up inside the hem, it is necessary to prick stitch fabric and lining together just below the hemline before the hem is turned up and finished. (For prick stitch see Dressmaking chapter 23, page 454.)

When sewing the inner edge of hems and bias facings to the mounted dress, make sure that you do not sew through to the outside fabric, but only catch the interlining fabric to give the outside a smooth finish.

If you follow all the instructions given for making bias facings and sewing hems, they will be secure and will not roll out.

Layouts for the shirt dress: Version C

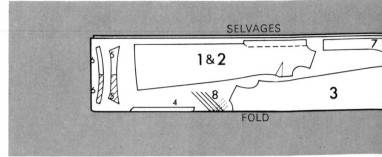

▲ *48in width, without one way, sizes 32½, 34, 36, 38, 40 & 42*
▼ *48in width, with one way, sizes 32½, 34, 36, 38, 40 & 42*

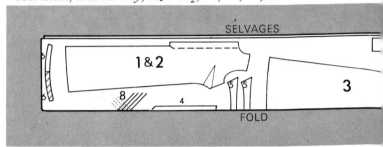

▼ *36in width, with and without one way, sizes 32½ & 34*

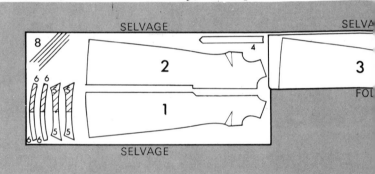

▼ *36in width, without one way, sizes 36, 38, 40 & 42*

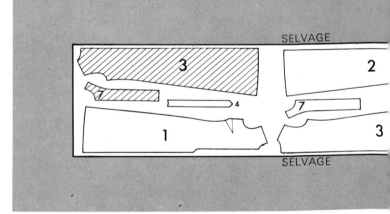

▼ *36in width, with one way, sizes 36, 38, 40 & 42*

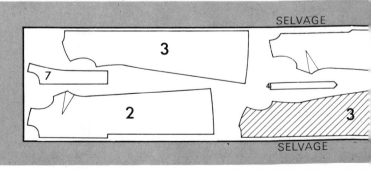

Version D

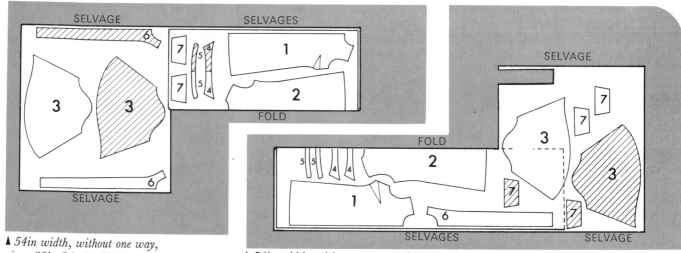

▲ *54in width, without one way,*
sizes 32½, 34, 36 & 38

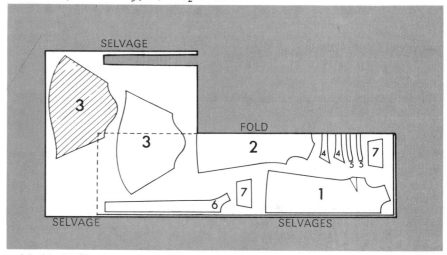

▲ *54in width, without one way, sizes 40 & 42*
▼ *54in width, with one way, sizes 32½ & 34*

Key to pattern pieces

Version C			**Version D**	
Right Front	=	1	Front	= 1
Left Front	=	2	Back	= 2
Back	=	3	Sleeve	= 3
Tab	=	4	Collar	= 4
Collar	=	5	Collar	
Collar band	=	6	band	= 5
Front facing	=	7	Front	
Bias strips	=	8	facing	= 6
			Cuff	= 7

Reverse pattern pieces ▨

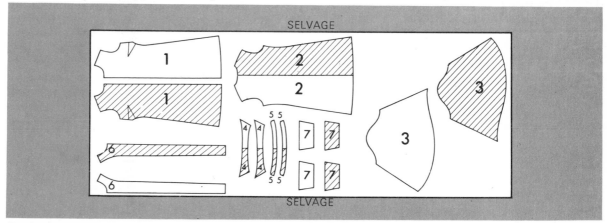

▼ *54in width, with one way, sizes 36, 38, 40 & 42*

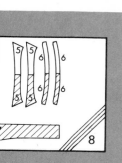

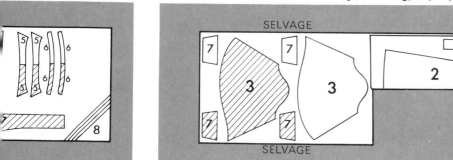

▼ *36in width, with and without one way, sizes 32½, 34, 36, 38, 40 & 42*

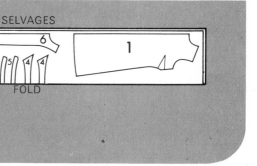

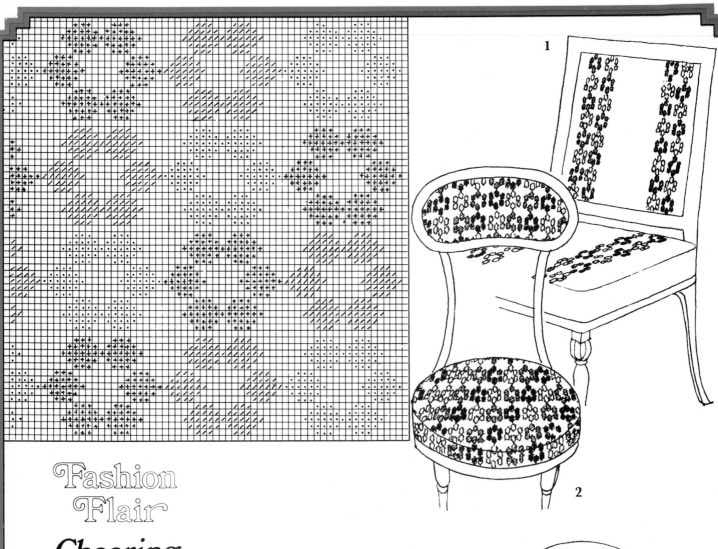

Fashion Flair

Cheering chairs

This geometric needlepoint can be used in several ways to create either traditional or modern, feminine or masculine effects, depending on whether it is an all-over pattern or worked in groups, and on the choice of colors and on the scale of the design.

1. *Double lines of motifs on a chair back line up with similar lines on the seat to give a strong, masculine look.*
2. *A close, all-over pattern achieves a traditional look.*
3. *Big, bold motifs in widely spaced lines give a modern look to an old fashioned chair.*
4. *A dainty, widely spaced all-over pattern makes a pretty chair for a feminine bedroom.*

Pattern Library

Little Polly Parasol

This demure little lady in her panniered dress and holding a pink parasol would make a pretty picture to frame. Work it in fine yarns such as 6-strand floss on a small mesh canvas. To decorate a pillow or a casual tote-bag, work the design in heavy yarns on a coarser canvas. Use either tent stitch or cross-stitch. The picture is slightly enlarged to be clear enough to use as a chart.

Stockings and socks, heels and toes

Knitting Know-how 44

Socks and stockings can be fashionable as well as practical accessories if well made and well finished. This chapter deals with the techniques of reinforcing, turning a heel and shaping a well fitting-toe.

Planning of stitches

Stockings and calf-length or knee socks usually require a certain amount of decreasing to shape a neat fitting ankle. The only exception to this is a ribbed stocking, where the fabric has a great deal of elasticity and stretches and contracts to fit the contours of the leg.

Where shaping is necessary, it is normally worked at either side of one or more center back stitches. The stitch, or stitches, between the decreases may even be worked in a stitch which contrasts with the surrounding fabric to produce a false seam effect.

When a patterned stitch is used for the leg, it is often worked beyond the ankle almost to the toe of the sock. It is best, however, if the pattern is only worked along the upper side of the instep and the heel, sole and upper and lower toe areas are worked in stockinette stitch for smoothness and comfort. The round toe shown on the opposite page is worked by decreasing stitches until just a few remain, and these are then threaded onto a strand of yarn and drawn up into a circle. Sometimes the toe is worked with decreasings at either side, and the remaining stitches are woven together so that there is no irritating seamline.

Dividing for the heel

When the leg length (either short or long) has been worked and the heel is reached, it is necessary to divide the stitches into two sections, one for the instep and one for the heel itself. A well-fitting sock usually has about the same number of stitches in both sections and, if the pattern will allow for it, it is better to have two stitches more on the instep than on the heel.

Reinforcing the heel

The heel is the first of these two sections to be worked. It is knitted back and forth in rows and may be worked in stockinette stitch, as shown here; however, as this part of the sock has to stand considerable friction, it is a good idea to strengthen the heel as you knit it to avoid future darning. This can be done by using a closer and finer stitch for the heel, such as a fabric stitch, or by knitting a fine nylon or nylon-silk sewing thread of matching color along with the yarn. A neat version is made by repeating the following 4 rows over the heel area.

Over an odd number of stitches, work:
1st row. K1, *sl 1, K1, rep from * to end.
2nd and 4th rows. P.
3rd row. K2, *sl 1, K1, rep from * to last st, K1.
Whichever method you choose, work until the heel section measures 2-2½in.

862

Turning the heel

To make a neat fitting heel which is not bulky and has a shaped section for the foot to fit into, it is necessary to divide the stitches into 3 sections. Work only on the middle section, working one stitch from each side into the center section until all the stitches are together again.

For example, if there are 39 stitches on the heel, 3 sections would consist of 13 stitches each. Work across the center 13 stitches, working the 13th stitch together with the next stitch from the side section, turn and work back across the center stitches again, working the last stitch together with the first one from the other side section. Continue in this way, back and forth, until all the stitches from the side sections have been worked into the center section. To return to circular knitting and to complete the foot, stitches are now picked up along either side of the heel and the stitches for the instep are brought back into use. The shaping required to reduce the number of stitches to the number needed for the foot is worked in two triangular sections at either side of the heel by decreasing one stitch at either side of the instep on each alternate row. The correct foot width is normally the same as the ankle width or, possibly, two stitches less.

Shaping the toe

The foot is worked until the point for the toe shaping is reached. If the instep has been patterned, this is a good point to finish the pattern because the toe is shaped more easily and is more comfortable to wear if it is worked in stockinette stitch.

A flat toe is worked by decreasing two stitches at either side of the toe width until a small number of stitches remain. These stitches are then divided and woven together.

A round toe is made by dividing the remaining stitches into 6 sections and working two stitches together at the end of each section. The rounded effect is obtained by gradually altering the number of rows between the decreasing rounds. With 6 stitches between the decreases, 6 rounds will be worked before the next decreasing round, and when 5 stitches are between sections 5 rounds are worked, and so on.

For example, if the total number of stitches is 54, then there will be 9 stitches in 6 sections.
1st dec round. *K7, K2 tog, rep from * to end. Work 7 rounds.
2nd dec round. *K6, K2 tog, rep from * to end. Work 6 rounds.
3rd dec round. *K5, K2 tog, rep from * to end. Work 5 rounds.
4th dec round. *K4, K2 tog, rep from * to end. Work 4 rounds.
5th dec round. *K3, K2 tog, rep from * to end. Work 3 rounds.
6th dec round. *K2, K2 tog, rep from * to end. Work 2 rounds.
7th dec round. *K1, K2 tog, rep from * to end. Work 1 round.
8th dec round. *K2 tog, rep from * to end.
Break yarn and thread through remaining stitches. Draw up and finish off on the wrong side.

Broken vertical rib suitable for sock patterns

Worked over a number of stitches divisible by 6.
1st, 3rd and 5th rows. *K3, P1 tbl, K2, rep from * to end.
2nd, 4th and 6th rows. *P2, K1 tbl, P3, rep from * to end.
7th, 9th and 11th rows. *P1 tbl, K5, rep from * to end.
8th, 10th and 12th rows. *P5, K1 tbl, rep from * to end.
These 12 rows form the pattern.

Horizontal rib suitable for sock patterns

Worked over an even number of stitches.
1st row. K.
2nd row. P.
3rd row. *K1, P1, rep from * to end.
4th row. K the K sts and P the P sts.
These 4 rows form the pattern.

▲ Shaping across center heel section

Completing the heel ▶

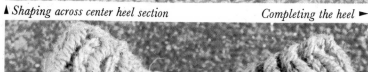

◀ Reverting to circular knitting after completion of heel

▲ Rounded toe ▼ Broken vertical rib ▼ Horizontal rib

Stockings with lovely lacy looks

Make these lacy stockings with an expensive look from two simple patterns.

Size
To fit a 10in foot (adjustable). Leg length, 34in.

Gauge
7 sts and 9 rows to 1in over stockinette stitch worked on No.3 needles

Materials
3-ply fingering yarn (1 oz. balls)
Daisy lace stockings 10 balls
One pair No. 5 needles (or Canadian No. 8)
Lace rib stockings 8 balls
One pair No. 3 needles (or Canadian No. 10)

Daisy lace stockings

Using No.5 needles, cast on 73 sts.

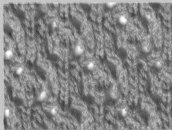

1st row *K1, P1, rep from * to last st, K1.
2nd row *P1, K1, rep from * to last st, P1.
Rep these 2 rows for 1½in. Commence patt.
Note Do not count sts on 3rd, 4th, 9th or 10th rows as extra sts are made in patt.
1st row *K1, ytf, sl 1, K1, psso, K1, K2 tog, ytf, rep from * to last st, K1.
2nd and every other row P.
3rd row *K2, ytf, K3, ytf, K1, rep from * to last st, K1.

5th row K2 tog, *ytf, sl 1, K1, psso, K1, K2 tog, ytf, sl 1, K2 tog, psso, rep from * to last 7 sts, ytf, sl 1, K1, psso, K1, K2 tog, ytf, sl 1, K1, psso.
7th row *K1, K2 tog, ytf, K1, ytf, sl 1, K1, psso, rep from * to last st, K1.
9th row As 3rd.
11th row *K1, K2 tog, ytf, sl 1, K2 tog, psso, ytf, sl 1, K1, psso, rep from * to last st, K1.
12th row P.
These 12 rows form patt. Continue in patt until work measures 14in from beg, ending with a P row.

Shape leg
Next row K2, sl 1, K1, psso, patt to last 4 sts, K2 tog, K2.
Work 7 rows without shaping. Keeping patt correct, dec one st at each end in this way on next and every following 8th row until 63 sts rem.
Continue without shaping until work measures 24in from beg.
Dec one st at each end inside 2 edge sts as before on next and every following 6th row until 45 sts rem.
Continue without shaping until work measures 32in from beg, ending with a 2nd, 6th, 8th or 12th patt row.

Shape heel
Next row K8 sts, turn, slip rem sts on holder.
Beg with a P row, work 13 rows st st on these 8 sts.
Next row K4, sl 1, K1, psso, turn.
Next row P.
Next row K4, sl 1, K1, psso, turn.

Next row P.
Next row K4, sl 1, K1, psso, pick up and K7 from side of heel, patt across rem 37 sts.
Next row P8, turn, slip rem sts on holder.
Beg with a K row, work 13 rows st st on these 8 sts.
Next row P4, P2 tog, turn.
Next row K.
Next row P4, P2 tog, turn.
Next row P.
Next row P4, P2 tog, pick up and P7 from side of heel, P across rem sts. 53 sts.
Keeping lace patt correct across center 29 sts for instep and working side panels in st st, work 4 rows.
Next row K11, K2 tog, patt 27 sts, sl 1, K1, psso, K to end. Work 3 rows.
Next row K10, K2 tog, patt 27 sts, sl 1, K1, psso, K to end. Work 3 rows.
Next row K9, K2 tog, patt 27 sts, sl 1, K1, psso, K to end. 47 sts.
Keeping panels correct, continue without shaping until work measures 7¼in from side of heel panels, or desired foot length less 1½in.

Shape toe
1st row K8, *K2 tog, K7, rep from * to last 3 sts, K2 tog, K1.
2nd and every other row P.
3rd row K7, *K2 tog, K6, rep from * to last 3 sts, K2 tog, K1.
5th row K6, *K2 tog, K5, rep from * to last 3 sts, K2 tog, K1.
7th row K5, *K2 tog, K4, rep from * to last 3 sts, K2 tog, K1.
9th row K4, *K2 tog, K3, rep from * to last 3 sts, K2 tog, K1.
11th row K3, *K2 tog, K2, rep from * to last 3 sts, K2 tog, K1.
13th row K2, *K2 tog, K1, rep from * to last 3 sts, K2 tog, K1. 12 sts.
Break yarn, thread through rem sts and fasten off securely.

Finishing

Press lightly on WS under a damp cloth with a warm iron. Using a flat st, join foot and

heel seams. Using backstitch, join leg seams. Press seams.

Lace rib stockings

Using No.3 needles, cast on 93 sts and work 1½in rib as given for daisy lace stockings. Commence patt.

1st row P2, *K2 tog, ytf, K1, ytf, sl 1, K1, psso, P2, rep from * to end.
2nd row K2, *P5, K2, rep from * to end.
These 2 rows form patt. Continue in patt until work measures 14in from beg, ending with a WS row.

Shape leg
Next row P2, sl 1, K1, psso, patt to last 4 sts, K2 tog, P2.
Next row K3, patt to last 3 sts, K3.
Keeping patt correct, dec one st at each end in this way on 7th and every following 8th row until 75 sts rem.
Continue without shaping until work measures 24in from beg.
Dec one st at each end inside 2 edge sts as before on next and every following 6th row until 53 sts rem.
Continue without shaping until work measures 32in from beg, ending with a WS row.

Shape heel
Next row K10 sts, turn and slip rem sts on holder.
Beg with a P row, work 15 rows st st on these 10 sts.
Next row K6, sl 1, K1, psso, turn.
Next row P.
Next row K6, sl 1, K1, psso, turn.
Next row P.
Next row K6, sl 1, K1, psso, pick up and K9 from side of heel, patt across rem 43 sts.
Next row P10 sts, turn and

slip rem sts on holder.
Beg with a K row, work 15
rows st st on these 10 sts.
Next row P6, P2 tog, turn.
Next row K.
Next row P6, P2 tog, turn.
Next row K.
Next row P6, P2 tog, pick up
and P9 from side of heel, work
in patt across sts on holder
to last 16 sts, P16. 65 sts.
Keeping lace patt correct
across center 33 sts for instep
and working side panels in
st st, work 4 rows.
Next row K14, K2 tog, patt
33 sts, sl 1, K1, psso, K to end.
Work 3 rows.
Next row K13, K2 tog, patt
33 sts, sl 1, K1, psso, K to end.
Work 3 rows.
Next row K12, K2 tog, patt
33 sts, sl 1, K1, psso, K to end.
Keeping panels correct,
continue without shaping
until work measures 7¼in from
side of heel, or desired foot
length less 1½in.

Shape toe
1st row K6, *K2 tog, K8,
rep from * to last 3 sts, K2
tog, K1.
2nd and every other row P.
3rd row K5, *K2 tog, K7,
rep from * to last 3 sts, K2
tog, K1.
5th row K4, *K2 tog, K6,
rep from * to last 3 sts, K2
tog, K1.
7th row K3, *K2 tog, K5,
rep from * to last 3 sts, K2
tog, K1.
9th row K2, *K2 tog, K4,
rep from * to last 3 sts, K2
tog, K1.
11th row K1, *K2 tog, K3,
rep from * to last 3 sts, K2
tog, K1.
13th row *K2 tog, K2, rep
from * to last 3 sts, K2 tog,
K1.
15th row *K2 tog, K1, rep
from * to last 2 sts, K2 tog.
1 sts.
Break yarn, thread through
sts, draw up and fasten off
securely.

Finishing

s for daisy lace stockings.

aisy lace pattern knitted in cream.
ce rib pattern in deep rose ➤

Crochet goes to headboards

▲ *Close-up detail of the motif for the headboard panel*

This beautiful headboard is a typical example of lacis crochet, which is derived from filet crochet and which originated in Germany. The crochet panel illustrated has been worked in lime green and mounted over foam padding covered in royal blue fabric. Work the panel in these colors or any others which suit your decor.

Size

13in wide by 36in long.

Materials

Clark's Big Ball Mercerized Crochet No. 10—4 balls
One No. B (2.00 mm) crochet hook
Foam padding 13 in. wide by 36 in. long by 3 in. thick
1yd of 45 in. wide fabric
Metal or bamboo rod to fit
Rings 1½ in. diameter if fabric tabs are not desired

Headboard in lacis crochet

Using No.B crochet hook, *ch4. Leaving last loop of each st on hook, work 2tr into 4th ch from hook, yoh and draw through all loops on hook (a 2tr cluster made), rep from * 40 times more. 41 clusters.

1st row Ch3, skip next cluster, 1tr into base of next cluster (sp made), *ch3, 1tr into base of next cluster, rep from * 37 times more, ch3,

leaving last loop of each st on hook work 3tr into base of next cluster, yoh and draw through all loops on hook (a 3tr cluster made). Turn. 40sp.

2nd row Ch4, 2tr cluster into 1st cluster, ch3, 1tr into next tr (sp made over sp), *3tr into next sp, 1tr into next tr, rep from * 37 times more (38 blocks made over 38sp), ch3, 3tr cluster into next cluster. Turn.

3rd row Ch4, 2tr cluster into 1st cluster, 1sp, 1tr into each of next 4tr (block made over block), *ch3, skip next 3 tr, 1tr into next tr, rep from * 35 times more (36sp made over 36 blocks), 1 block, ch3, 3tr cluster into next cluster. Turn.

4th row Ch4, 2tr cluster into 1st cluster, 1sp, 1 block, 36 sp, 1 block, ch3, 3tr cluster into next cluster. Turn.

5th row Ch4, 2tr cluster into 1st cluster, 1sp, 1 block, 2sp, *3tr cluster into next tr, (ch4, 2tr cluster into 4th ch from hook) twice, 3tr cluster into same place as last 3tr cluster (diamond cluster made), 1tr into next tr, rep from * twice more, ch4, 2tr cluster into 4th ch from hook (cluster bar made), 1tr into next tr, 8sp, ch3, 3tr cluster into next tr, follow diagram to end of row. Turn.

6th row Ch4, 2tr cluster into 1st cluster, 1sp, 1 block, 2sp, (ch3, 1sc into center ch of next diamond cluster, ch3, 1tr into next tr) 3 times, ch3, 1tr into next tr, 6sp, diamond cluster into next tr, 1tr into next tr, diamond

Diagram for working the lacis crochet headboard panel

cluster into next cluster, follow diagram to end of row. Turn.

7th row Ch4, 2tr cluster into 1st cluster, 1sp, 1 block, 2sp, (diamond cluster into next sc, 1tr into next tr) twice, follow diagram to end of row. Turn.

8th row Ch4, follow diagram to end of row. Turn.

9th row Ch4, 2tr cluster into 1st cluster, 1sp, 1 block, 2sp, diamond cluster into next sc, 1tr into next tr, 9sp, ch3, 1sc into center ch

of next diamond cluster, ch3, 1tr into next tr, 1sp, *skip 2ch, 1tr into next ch, ch1, inserting hook from behind last tr work 1tr into first of 2 skipped ch (cross made), 1tr into next tr, rep from * 3 times more, .1sp, follow diagram to end of row. Turn.

10th row Ch4, 2tr cluster into 1st cluster, 1sp, 1 block, 2sp, ch3, 1sc into center ch of next diamond cluster, ch3, 1tr into next tr, 7sp, diamond cluster into next tr, 1tr into next tr, 2sp,

acis crochet in lime green over royal blue gives a bright, crisp effect for modern bedroom decor

diamond cluster into next
, skip 2tr, 1tr into next
, skip 2tr) twice, diamond
uster into next tr (3
amond clusters made over 4
oss sts), follow diagram to
d of row. Turn.

th row Ch4, follow diagram
end of row. Turn.

th row Ch4, 2tr cluster
to first cluster, 1sp, 1 block,
sp, diamond cluster into
xt sc, 1tr into next tr,
p, skip next tr, 1tr into
xt tr, ch1, inserting hook
m behind last tr work 1tr

into tr just skipped (cross
st made over cross st), 1tr
into next tr, follow diagram
to end of row. Turn.
Beg each row with ch4,
follow diagram to top, turn
diagram and omitting last 2
rows, follow diagram back to
1st row. Fasten off.

Finishing

Dampen crochet and pin out
to measurements.
Cut fabric for covering foam,
noting that ½in has been

allowed on all sides for seams.
Cut 2 pieces 14in by 37in for
front and back.
Cut 2 pieces 4in by 37in and
2 pieces 4in by 14in for
gussets.
Cut 5 pieces 4in by 8in for
tabs, if preferred instead of
rings. Fold tab pieces in half
lengthwise and st long edges.
Turn to RS.
Join 1 long gusset piece to 1
short gusset piece by machine
stitching short ends. Join rem
2 gussets in same way. Join 2
sections tog to form rectangle,

machine stitching across free
short ends.
Place front section on gussets,
edges even, RS tog and
machine st all around.
Place and baste tabs in
position to RS of back section,
raw edges tog. Place
long edge with tabs on gussets,
RS tog and machine st.
Trim seams, turn to RS and
insert pad. Turn in rem seam
allowance on back section and
sl st to gussets.
Sew crocheted piece in place
on front of completed pad.

Fantasy in black and gold

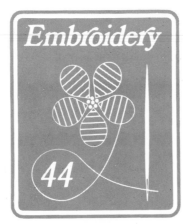

This intriguing Eastern fantasy panel uses a modern interpretation of the ancient form of embroidery known as blackwork. The completed effect is simply a build-up of straight and simple stitches. Each individual building on the panel is a complete design in itself and can be used on its own.

On the following pages is an almost life-size reproduction of the Eastern panel with a scale below indicating the number of threads. The panel can be used as a chart from which to work.

Materials you will need

- ☐ ½yd 59 inch wide even-weave linen with 21 threads to the inch (finished size of panel 23½ inches by 13½ inches)
- ☐ 6 skeins black six-strand floss
- ☐ 1 spool Penelope metallic gold cord
- ☐ 3 cards Penelope gold lurex
- ☐ 1 card Penelope silver lurex
- ☐ Tapestry needle size 22 (for working gold and silver threads)
- ☐ Tapestry needle size 26 (for working six-strand floss)
- ☐ Hardboard 23½ inches by 13½ inches
- ☐ Embroidery frame

Working from the two-page chart

This is a counted thread design and the stitches are worked over the counted threads of the fabric. The almost life-size picture of the panel on the following pages can therefore

be used as a working chart. The diagrams show how some of the more complicated filling patterns are built up, and these are numbered to identify them with the areas to be worked in the patterns on the outline diagram. Each grid line of the filling pattern diagrams represents one thread of the fabric.

Using the threads

Six-strand floss. Use two strands for the filling patterns and outlines, one strand for the paving, and four strands on the towers of the left-hand building.

Gold and silver lurex. Use single for stitching, double for couching.

Metallic gold cord. Use double throughout.

Stitches in the design

Outlines

In blackwork, the outline is worked before the filling patterns. The main outline stitch in this design is whipped backstitch worked in 6-strand floss. Other outline effects are as follows:

Couched gold. Two lengths of couched gold lurex thread are caught down with one thread of 6-strand floss on the large towers of the left-hand building and on the outline of the center front roof of the right-hand building.

Whipped backstitch. This is worked entirely in gold lurex on the base of the large towers of the left-hand building, around the diamond shape on the center roof of the same building, on the side turrets and the

top center dome of the center building, and around the large dome of the right-hand building.

A row of backstitch is worked over as shown in the diagram, using either a self color or a contrasting color.

Double whipped backstitch. Black backstitch with gold lurex whipping on the side domes of the right-hand building.

This is worked in the same way as whipped backstitch, and a second row of whip stitches is worked back along the line of backstitches in the opposite direction.

Backstitch. This is worked on the edge of the section immediately below the domes on the right-hand building.

Pekinese stitch. This is worked with black backstitch and gold lurex interlacing on the center section of the large dome on the center building. A foundation line of small backstitches has a second thread looped through. Do not carry second thread to back of work except at beginning and end of row.

Filling stitches

Pattern fillings are worked after the outline has been completed and consist of straight stitches worked over counted threads. The two smaller rounded towers and the doors of the large building are worked in double cross-stitch. The filling pattern on the large central dome consists of satin stitch blocks worked and interlaced with metallic gold cord.

Threaded satin stitch. The blocks of satin stitch are threaded through in zigzag fashion using self or contrasting color thread.

Mounting the panel

When the embroidery is completed, remove it from the frame and press lightly on the back of the work using a dry cloth to protect the metal threads from heat. Mount the panel on a piece of hardboard, as described in Embroidery chapter 19, page 366.

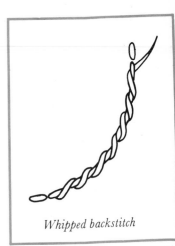

Whipped backstitch

Double whipped backstitch

Pekinese stitch

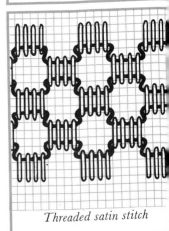

Threaded satin stitch

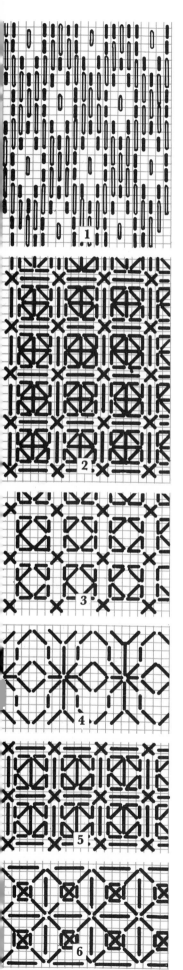

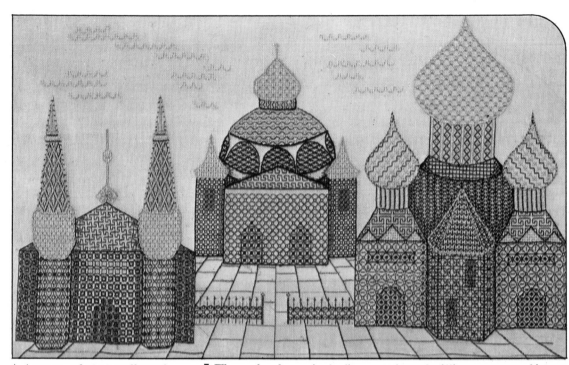

▲ *An eastern fantasy wall panel*   ▼ *The numbered areas in the diagram refer to the filling patterns on this page*

0 20 30 40 50 60 70 80 90 100 110 120 130 140 150 160 170 180 190 200 210 220 230

Each mark on the scale indicates every tenth thread on the fabric
870

Seat cushions

Make a seat cushion or two and add an individual touch to your dining room or kitchen chairs. Full instructions are given in this chapter for making cushions with piped seams and an elastic anchor strip. A method of finishing with tapes and zipper is also described, plus instructions for buttoning.

Making the pattern

You will need

- ☐ Sheet of newspaper
- ☐ Sheet of heavy brown paper
- ☐ Scissors to cut the paper
- ☐ Pencil

A cushion should be the same shape as the chair seat which it covers.

Lay the sheet of newspaper across the chair seat and press it down around the front and side edges of the seat. At the back edge of the seat, fold the newspaper toward you and make a crease along the back edge of the chair or, if the chair has struts at the back, along the line of struts where they meet the seat. Cut out the newspaper pattern along the creases, shaping it where necessary to fit around the side struts.

Check that the pattern fits the seat exactly. If you need to make sure that the pattern is symmetrical, fold it in half lengthwise and see if the cut edges match each other.

When you are satisfied that the newspaper pattern is correct, place it on the brown paper and cut out exactly the same shape. This pattern is without seam allowance.

The pad

You will need

- ☐ A sheet of foam rubber 1 inch thick, slightly larger than the chair seat.
- ☐ A fairly large pair of sharp scissors
- ☐ A ball point pen
- ☐ Masking tape (available from most stationery or hobby stores)
- ☐ The brown paper pattern

Lay the pattern onto the sheet of foam rubber and anchor it with small pieces of masking tape. Draw carefully around the pattern with the ball point pen. Pull off masking tape, remove pattern and cut out foam rubber pad along pen line.

The cover

Suitable fabrics

Seat cushions receive a lot of wear, so you must choose a fabric which is firm and will not pull or stretch at the seams. Linen, cotton and some synthetics are all washable, while upholstery velvet, corduroy and tweed wear very well but should be dry cleaned.

You will need

For a seat cushion with piped seams, a slip stitched opening and elastic anchor strip:
- ☐ Fabric. The amount depends on the size of the chair seat, plus what you will need for covering the piping cord, but as a general rule 1 yard of 36 inch wide fabric will be enough for an average sized cushion
- ☐ Sewing and basting thread
- ☐ A length of piping cord

equal to the perimeter of the cushion, plus 1 inch
- ☐ A length of ½ inch wide elastic equal to the width of the cushion at the back
- ☐ A large snap fastener
- ☐ The brown paper pattern

Making the cover

Fold the fabric, right sides facing, to accommodate the pattern with at least ½ inch of fabric showing all around the pattern.

Pin on the pattern, mark around the edge for the stitching line and then mark a ½ inch seam allowance. Unpin the pattern and cut out the cover.

Cut bias strips 1½ inches wide from the remaining fabric and join them together, as shown in figure 1, to the length of the piping cord.

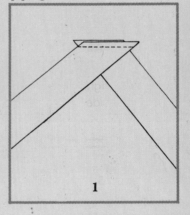

1

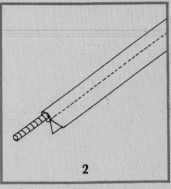

2

Cover the piping cord as shown in figure 2, stitching it with a zipper foot on the sewing machine.

Baste the piping to the right side of one of the cover pieces, as shown in Home Sewing chapter 2, page 288, with the stitching line of the piping matching the stitching line on the fabric piece. Stitch the piping in position. Place the other cover piece onto the piped piece, right sides facing, and stitch them together along the stitching line for the piping. Stitch along three sides only, leaving back edge open. Turn cover right side out.

Insert the foam rubber pad into the cover and close the opening with slip stitch.

To secure the cushion to the chair, sew the socket half of the snap to the left-hand back corner on the underside

Round cushion in a print   *A buttoned cushion*

of the cushion, and the elastic to the right-hand back corner. Turn under and sew the free end of the elastic and sew the ball half of the snap to the finished end (figure **3**).

Place the cushion in position on the chair, pass the elastic under the chair seat and close the snap fastener.

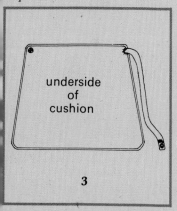

3

Tapes and zipper finish

You will need
- [ ] The brown paper pattern
- [ ] Foam rubber pad
- [ ] Cover fabric
- [ ] Piping cord
- [ ] Sewing and basting thread
- [ ] 1 yard $\frac{1}{2}$ inch wide straight tape (in a matching color)
- [ ] A zipper, 2 inches less in length than the width of the back edge of the cushion

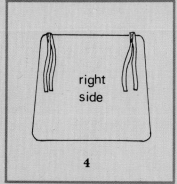

4

Fold the fabric, cut and mark the cover pieces and cover the piping cord as before.

Cut the straight tape into two 18 inch lengths and fold each of these in half. Place the tapes on the right side of one of the cover pieces as shown in figure **4**, and pin.

Baste on the piping cord so that the tapes are sandwiched between the piping and the

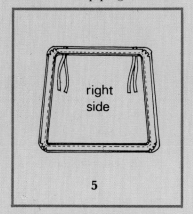

5

cover (figure **5**). Insert one half of the zipper as described in Home Sewing chapter 2, page 288, then stitch piping, tapes and zipper in one operation. Baste and stitch the other half of the zipper in position, join the cover pieces and turn the cover right side out.

Using matching ties
Instead of straight tape it is a pretty idea to use matching ties made of the cover fabric. Cut a long strip from the cover fabric 2 inches wide and 36 inches long, fold this in half lengthwise, right sides facing, and stitch along the length. Turn the strip of fabric right side out, cut it in half so that you have two 18 inch lengths and finish all the ends. Stitch the strips to the cover as shown in the instructions for the straight tapes.

Buttoned cushions

You will need
- [ ] Five $\frac{3}{4}$in button molds
- [ ] Five $\frac{1}{2}$in shirt buttons
- [ ] Scraps of the cover fabric for covering the button molds
- [ ] Button and basting thread

Decide where you wish the buttons to be placed and mark these points with basting thread

on each side of the cushion. Cover the button molds with fabric. Place each covered button in the correct position on the upper side of the cushion and a small button on the underside directly beneath the top button. Sew the covered button to the small button through the pad with several

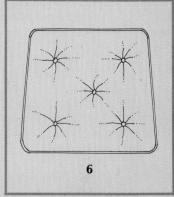

6

firm stitches, pulling the thread taut as you sew. Fasten off securely on the underside of the cushion (figure **6**).

Handy hint
To remove the cover for washing or cleaning, simply snip the threads below the small buttons and remove all the buttons. The cover will then slip off easily and it is an extremely simple matter to sew on the buttons again when the cover is replaced.

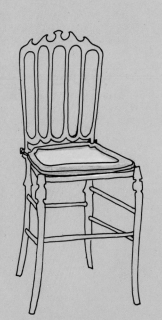

Cushion in contrasting colors

Cushion in a simple check

Cushion with bold appliqué

Plain cushion in a bold color

Variations on bishop sleeves

This chapter is all about the bishop sleeve which is full, soft and glamorous. It is shown here with deep, tapered cuffs and rouleau fastenings.

The bishop sleeve is an adaptation of the shirt sleeve in the Creative Hands Pattern Pack. The variations sketched here show how it can be combined with Creative Hands blouse and dress patterns to give you a variety of looks. You'll also see from this chapter how to adapt the bishop sleeve pattern itself in some very exciting ways.

The chapter starts off with full instructions for making the bishop sleeve with rouleau fastening for the shirt dress version D, for which yardages and details are given on page 876. For this version, choose a soft type of fabric to do justice to the lovely, full sleeve shape, but make sure that the fabric is crease resistant or the sleeves will not look their best at all times. For a special occasion choose a printed chiffon, mount the Front and Back, collar and cuffs onto taffeta and use the chiffon on its own for the sleeves. Most printed chiffons have a little more texture than the plain ones and are easier to use than very delicate fabric.

The bishop sleeve

The sleeve pattern

First make sure you have some large sheets of paper for making new patterns.

You will need the shirt sleeve pattern piece number 8 from the accessory sheet in the Creative Hands Pattern Pack.

Copy the sleeve pattern and all its markings.

Slash the pattern as shown (figure **1**). First slash along the center, then make three slashes equally spaced on each side of the first one. Make them all to within a fraction of the sleeve cap, which must remain intact.

To spread the pattern you need a sheet of paper 36 inches wide and the length of the sleeve pattern. Draw the lengthwise straight of grain down the center of the paper.

Place the slashed pattern on the paper, spread the center slash 1 inch on each side of the grain line and spread each side slash 2 inches apart.

Pin all sections of the pattern securely in place, then extend the sleeve seams 3 inches on each side at the wrist edge, as shown. This gives a lovely full sleeve which is ideal for fine fabrics. If you are using a heavier fabric, you may prefer less fullness, in which case simply spread the pattern less and omit the extension on the side seams.

Draw the new pattern carefully, shaping the wrist edge and tapering the sleeves seams correctly. Mark the opening. Also transfer the markings on the sleeve cap.

Cut out the new pattern.

From left to right— bishop sleeve with: tie-neck blouse and jumper; tie-neck tunic; shirt with collar band finish; basic open-neck blouse; rouleau loop fastened dress

▼**1.** *Spreading the shirt sleeve pattern for the full bishop sleeve*

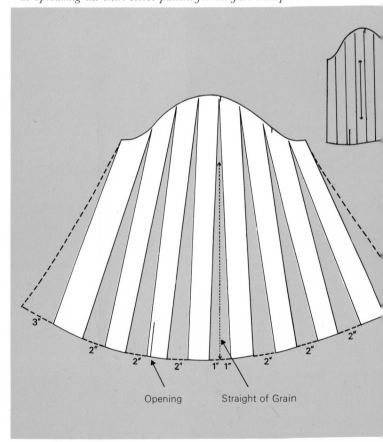

Opening   Straight of Grain

The cuff pattern

To make the new deep, shaped cuff, first copy the shirt cuff (pattern piece number 12 from the accessory sheet) onto paper. Mark the center of the cuff as shown in figure **2**, then measure your wrist. Allow $\frac{1}{2}$ inch for ease and mark this measurement centrally on one cuff edge as shown. The depth of the cuff pattern is $4\frac{1}{2}$ inches, so measure your arm $4\frac{1}{2}$ inches above the wrist, add 1 inch for ease, and mark off on the opposite, top edge of the cuff. Taper the sides of the cuff toward the wrist, add $\frac{3}{4}$ inch on one end for the wrap.

Helpful hints

Make the bishop sleeve with a rolled opening (see Dressmaking chapter 41, page 814). Cut two fabric sections for each cuff and interface the top section.

It is essential that you buy the buttons before you start making the cuffs. This is because the cuffs are fastened with rouleau loops and buttons and the size of the loops is determined by the size of the buttons. For loop fastening high-domed, covered buttons are the most attractive (many stores provide a button-covering service). Alternatively, the ball type, such as pearl buttons, may also be used.

▼**2.** *Making the tapered cuff pattern for the full bishop sleeve*

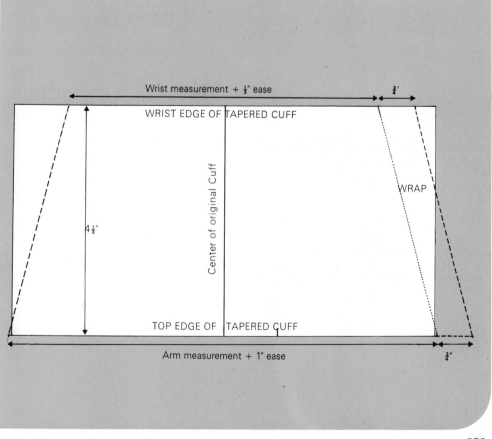

Wrist measurement + $\frac{1}{2}$″ ease $\frac{3}{4}$″

WRIST EDGE OF TAPERED CUFF

Center of original Cuff

$4\frac{1}{2}$″

WRAP

TOP EDGE OF TAPERED CUFF

Arm measurement + 1″ ease $\frac{3}{4}$″

Making the rouleau loops

For the loops, first make a $\frac{1}{8}$ inch wide rouleau.

Cut a bias strip four times the width of the finished rouleau (that is, $\frac{1}{2}$ inch wide). The length of the bias strip depends on the size and number of buttons you are using. For a quick, and safe, calculation measure over the dome of the button, add $1\frac{1}{2}$ inches to this measurement and multiply by the number of buttons to be used.

Make the rouleau as shown.

Attaching the loops

To find the length of each rouleau loop, take the dome measurement of one button, add $\frac{1}{2}$ inch at each end for seam allowance, and cut the loops to that size.

To find the correct spacing for the loops on the cuff edge, pin one loop to the top, interfaced, section (right side) and button it. If it is correct, measure out equal spacings along the cuff edge, allowing for the thickness of the rouleau on both sides of each loop (figure **3**).

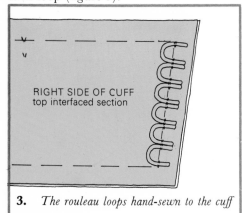

3. *The rouleau loops hand-sewn to the cuff*

Sew the loops in place by hand first, as shown.

Place the top, interfaced, and lower cuff sections together, right sides facing, then baste and stitch along the sides and wrist edge, leaving the top edge open.

Trim the seam allowance and snip across the corners, then turn the cuff to the right side, edge-baste and press (figure **4**). Do not press the loops.

If you find that the fabric you are using is not suitable for rouleau loops, use rat tail braid, applied as above, or hand-

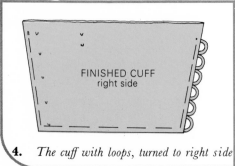

4. *The cuff with loops, turned to right side*

made loops. Work handmade loops (Dressmaking chapter 21, page 466) to fit the button size along the finished edge.

Finishing the cuff

With right sides facing, baste and stitch the open edge of the top, interfaced, cuff piece to the wrist edge of the sleeve. Make sure that the loops go to the top of the sleeve—that is, to the end of the opening furthest from the sleeve seam

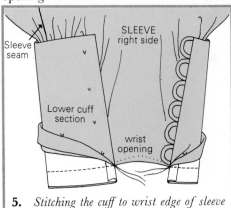

5. *Stitching the cuff to wrist edge of sleeve*

(figure **5**).

Trim the seam allowance and press the seam into the cuff.

Fold under the seam allowance of the remaining raw edge and slip stitch it in place over the stitching line on the inside of the sleeve. Press the sewn inside edge. Sew on the buttons opposite the loops, spacing them evenly.

Stitching on ball buttons

For loop fastening sew on ball buttons firmly, but for buttonholes sew on ball buttons loosely (but without a shank) to allow them to settle into the round ends. If they are sewed on too tightly, they will slip out of the buttonholes.

D. Shirt dress with bishop sleeves

Make this shirt dress like the shirt dress version A in Dressmaking chapter 42, page 834, but with the full, bishop sleeve. Layouts for this dress are in Dressmaking chapter 43, page 856.

Yardages
54in width. Without one way—size $32\frac{1}{2}$, $3\frac{1}{8}$ yards; sizes 34 and 36, $3\frac{1}{4}$ yards; sizes 38 and 40, $3\frac{3}{8}$ yards; size 42, $3\frac{1}{2}$ yards.
54in width. With one way—size $32\frac{1}{2}$, $3\frac{1}{4}$ yards; size 34, $3\frac{3}{8}$ yards; sizes 36, 38 and 40, $3\frac{7}{8}$ yards; size 42, 4 yards.
36in width. With and without one way—sizes $32\frac{1}{2}$ and 34, $4\frac{5}{8}$ yards; size 36, $4\frac{3}{4}$ yards; size 38, $4\frac{7}{8}$ yards; size 40, 5 yards; size 42, $5\frac{1}{4}$ yards.

Making a rouleau

Tips. Before cutting the bias strip for a rouleau, experiment to find the correct width for the type of fabric you are using. You should have enough seam allowance to fill the tubing, and the heavier the fabric, the narrower the seam allowance.

Avoid using fabrics which fray easily.

Technique. Cut the bias strip to the length and width required and fold lengthwise, right sides facing.

Machine stitch twice leaving threads 10 inches long. Thread these through a darning needle and knot securely (figure A).

Insert the eye of the needle into the fabric tube as shown and gently start to push the rouleau back over the needle so that, by careful pushing and pulling of the thread, the rouleau is turned to the right side (figure B). Roll the finished rouleau between your fingers, gently stretching it and making sure that the seam goes along one side.

Bishop sleeve variations

A. Full sleeve without cuff

The fullness in this sleeve is held in with an elastic casing or a bound rouleau finish.

The pattern. Use the bishop sleeve in figure **1**, but lengthen it to compensate for the cuff.

To do this cut across the pattern horizontally, halfway between underarm and wrist. Spread the pattern and draw in the new lines as shown (figure **6**).

Elastic casing. Make an elastic casing on the wrist edge as for the child's dress version B in Dressmaking chapter 38, pg. 75

Bound rouleau finish. Prepare a roll opening at the wrist as for the bishop sleeve and gather the wrist edge similarly. Cut a bias strip to your wrist measurement plus 2 inches, and four times the required width of the finished rouleau.

Bind the gathered edge leaving the 2 inch extension on the top of the sleeve. Fold the extension and slip stitch the edges together to give a neat finish.

Form a loop with the extension and sew

button on the opposite end of the opening to complete the fastening.

B. Gathered sleeve crown
The pattern. Slash the bishop sleeve pattern as shown (figure 7) and draw in the new lines.

The armhole line for this sleeve is set higher on the shoulder, so work out how much you will move it in, then raise the crown by this amount plus $\frac{1}{2}$ inch for ease. When setting in the sleeve, start the gathers about $4\frac{1}{2}$ inches on each side of the balance mark which falls on the shoulder seam, drawing up the gathers as close as possible.

C. The full sleeve with fitted top
The top of this sleeve is the same width as the basic shirt sleeve but extra width is added to the lower part.

The pattern. Copy the shirt sleeve pattern piece, number 8 on the accessory sheet. Following the diagram (figure 8), slash the pattern horizontally halfway between the underarm and elbow and a third of the way into the sleeve on both sides of the sleeve seam.

Next, slash the lower section vertically, in line with the inner ends of the horizontal slashes.

Make one or two more vertical slashes on each side of the sleeve between the first slash and the sleeve seam, depending on how full you want the sleeve. Spread the vertical slashes. The sides will rise above the horizontal cuts, so add the amount by which they overlap to the wrist edge of the sleeve seam. Draw in the new lines.

D. Sleeve with frilled wrist
This can be gathered with elastic and a self-casing on the inside of the sleeve, or it can be drawn up with cord or ribbon slotted into a casing on the outside of the sleeve. You can use self fabric or contrasting lace or braid.

The pattern. Use the bishop sleeve pattern in figure 1, but without the extra extension on the sleeve seams.

To compensate for the cuff, extend the pattern downward by the amount required and use the original wrist edge as a guideline to stitch on the casing (figure 9).

Inside casing. Make a bias strip casing on the inside of the sleeve as for the child's dress version B in Dressmaking 38, page 6, and slot with elastic. Finish hem.

Outside casing. Make a casing on the outside of the sleeve with lace, braid or self fabric.

Leave the opening in the casing on the top of the sleeve for the ribbon ties. Or, if you prefer, you can make small buttonholes on each side of the opening to slot the ribbon through. Finish hem.

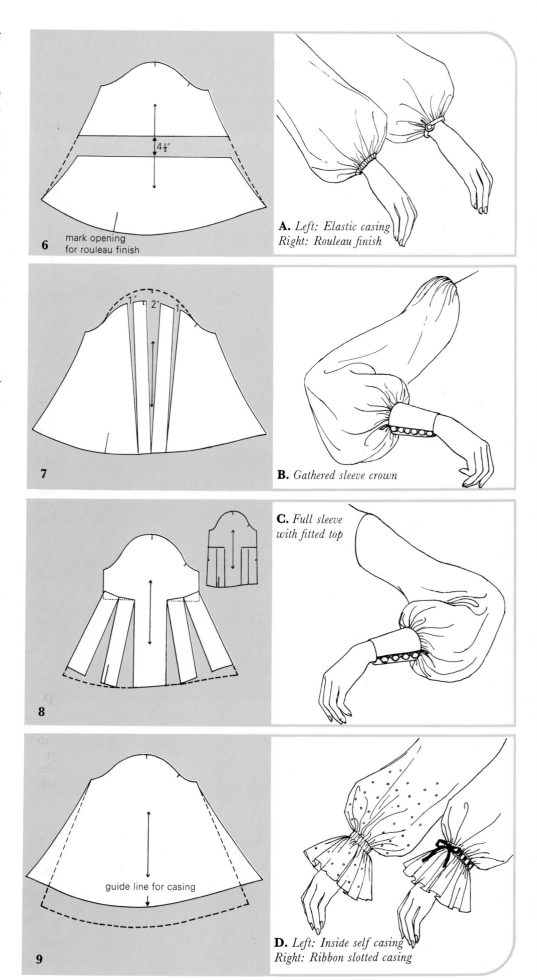

6 mark opening for rouleau finish

A. *Left: Elastic casing*
Right: Rouleau finish

7

B. *Gathered sleeve crown*

8

C. *Full sleeve with fitted top*

9 guide line for casing

D. *Left: Inside self casing*
Right: Ribbon slotted casing

Darn that hole!

Nothing is more irritating than a hole appearing in a perfectly good shirt, or to see a tear in your favorite skirt. But a stitch in time really does save nine and a neatly done mend is very rewarding. The two main methods of repairing are darning and patching. Darning creates a new piece of fabric to fill a hole or strengthen a thin place. This chapter explains various methods of darning for different holes and fabrics.

The method of repair and the yarn or thread for the job should be chosen carefully, bearing in mind the type of garment and the fabric involved. Generally, darning threads should be the same thickness, color and texture as the threads of the fabric. For some types of darning—reweaving for example—darning threads are drawn from a seam in a hidden part of the garment. Double length darning needles are recommended for all types of darning and should be as fine as possible.

Weft and warp threads

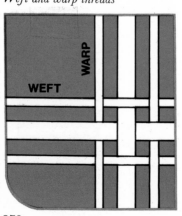

Reinforcing darns

These darns are worked to strengthen threads which already exist but have worn thin. Darn across the weft threads only, unless the area has worn so thin that this would not give adequate support.

In reinforcing darning, stitching is worked on the wrong side of the fabric. Small running stitches are worked back and forth across the thin area, keeping the rows of stitches as close as possible. If the darn is being worked on woolen fabric, using wool yarn, leave small loops at the end of each row to allow for shrinkage.

Web darning

Web darns are worked on woven and knitted fabrics to repair small and medium sized holes. This type of darn is easier to work if a darning egg is used.

Trim the edges of the hole, keeping it as small as possible. Working on the right side, begin darning outside the hole, reinforcing the surrounding area. The hole itself is filled in with newly woven threads. Work the warp threads first, making sure that the darning thread is worked over and under the edges of the hole on each alternate row.

When the warp way darning is completed, turn the work and darn the weft way, passing the needle over and then under the warp threads, as illustrated in the diagram, continuing the reinforcing darning into the area of fabric edging the hole.

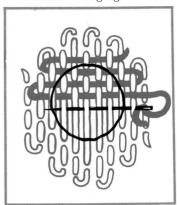

Catch tear darns

Catch tears are usually caused by accident, and there is no surrounding worn part to be reinforced. If the tear is large and jagged it will need patching, but a clean three-cornered, or straight, tear can be darned satisfactorily. Human hair is sometimes used for mending simple catch tears on very fine fabrics—this is termed stoteing—but it is not recommended on articles where there is likely to be a strain on the darn. Fine gauge, colorless nylon thread can be used for stoteing. Before darning, the edges of catch tears are drawn together with fishbone stitch. Fishbone stitch can be used for mending tears without further darning if the slit is very small.

To work fishbone stitch. Working on the wrong side of the fabric, fasten the thread with a few running stitches at one end of the tear and then pass the needle, from the back, through on one side of the slit about $\frac{1}{8}$in from it. Take the needle through the slit and bring it through, from the back on the other side of the slit.

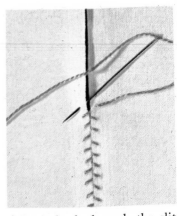

Take it back through the slit again, this time passing it over the previous stitch which lies in the center of the slit, thus pulling the stitch down.

Preparing the darn. Once the edges of the tear have been drawn together, the shape of the darn should be planned so that the weakest part of the fabric surrounding the tear is reinforced. The finished darn should cover an area about $\frac{1}{4}$in outside all the edges of the tear. Following the diagram, outline the area of the darn with basting stitches.

The three-cornered tear

Baste the outline of the darn shape. Working on the wrong side of the fabric, fishbone stitch the tear to draw the edges together. Holding the left hand thumb over the tear to prevent fraying while working, work the weft way first, from point **A** to **B** in the diagram, using small running stitches and stitching across the slit. Keep the stitches even and within the basted area. Work almost to the corner of the tear and slip the needle off the thread, leaving the end free.

Turn the work and, working from points **C** to **D** in the dia

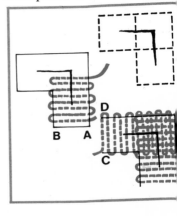

gram, stitch warp ways toward the corner of the tear. When the corner point is reached, leave the end of the thread free. Rethread the needle with the first hanging thread and finish working the weft way stitches across the corner. Then finish stitching with the second thread until the corner of the darn is completed. By working in this way, the grain of the fabric is kept symmetrical and this strengthens the weakest part of the tear.

Cross cut darn

If the tear or a cut has been made across the grain of the fabric, plan the darn as shown in the diagrams and, working as before, darn the shape marked **ABCD** and then darn shape **ECFA**. The double reinforcing darn forms a square over the cut or tear. In cross cut darning, the warp way is worked first.

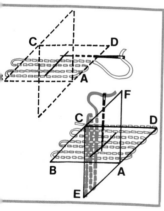

Reweaving darns

Darns involving the reweaving [of] fabric to fill a hole are usually worked on woven fabrics. The finished darn, if properly done, is almost invisible and is suitable for mending "best" clothes.

Study the weave of the fabric through a magnifying glass before starting to darn, so that you can duplicate it with your stitches. Threads for reweaving darns are drawn from an unseen part of the garment, such as a hem, but if you are working on a patterned fabric both warp and weft threads of each colour in the pattern will have to be drawn. Short lengths of

▲ *Reweaving a small hole*

▲▼ *Reweaving on patterned fabric*

thread can be used for reweaving as, on each row of darning, the ends of the threads are left free and a new thread used to begin next row. Place the work in an embroidery hoop to hold the fabric taut, wrong side up. Working from the area outside the hole, stitch the darning thread through the fabric, working over and under the existing threads and then across the hole. After completing the darning one way, turn the work and darn the other way. Make sure that the needle is passed through the darning threads in exactly the same way

Reweaving an uneven weave fabric

as the fabric is woven (see diagram). After the hole has been filled, clip the ends of the thread $\frac{1}{8}$in from the surface of the fabric. Press the mend.

A smoother surface and more professional looking invisible mend can be achieved by unpicking the original broken threads back from the hole as each new thread is darned in. The broken threads are unpicked to an irregular shape and these threads are trimmed off after the darn is completed.

Reweaving a clean cut

A clean cut or a catch tear without a surrounding worn area can be mended almost invisibly with a woven darn. Close the edges of the tear with fishbone stitch. Using threads drawn from the inside of the garment or from a similar piece of fabric darn across the slit, working on the wrong side, using the reweaving method and working over an area of about $\frac{1}{2}$in on each side.

Darning on net

Holes in net are darned by duplicating the formation of the net itself, using closely matched thread.

Following the diagrams, begin by working the horizontal threads, making sure that the stitches are worked beyond the width of the damaged part by at least two holes at each end. The second stage of the darn is worked from left to right, beginning two holes below the bottom row of horizontal threads. Loop the thread once around each of the horizontal threads (see diagram **2**) working diagonally upward. The last stage of darning is worked from left to right, beginning two holes above the top row of horizontal threads, and working diagonally toward the bottom thread. Finish thread off firmly. This method produces an almost invisible mend.

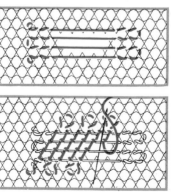

for repairing tears when a pocket is ripped, for a torn opening on a garment, or for split seams or gussets. It can also be used generally for strengthening worn places on household linen and towels.

Combined patch and machine darn

Draw the edges of the tear together using fishbone stitch. Cut a piece of fabric of similar weight and texture to back the tear. Tape can be used for backing some fabrics but only when the weight matches and when the garment is made of non-stretch fabric.

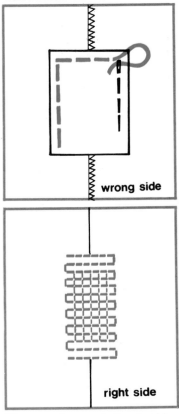

wrong side

right side

Net can be used for backing thin fabrics and forms a light yet adequate support.

Trim the backing fabric so that it covers the tear with $\frac{1}{2}$in to spare all around. Baste the backing to the wrong side of the garment after the fishboning has been worked.

Working on the right side, machine stitch back and forth across the tear or worn place in rows about $\frac{1}{4}$in apart (see diagram). This is usually sufficient to make a good repair, but if further strengthening is required, work in the opposite direction as well. Trim the raw

edges of the backing fabric on the wrong side, close to the machine stitching, and then over-cast the edges. Press the mend.

Free machine darning

Free machine darning produce a strong darn, but it is not recommended for mending cloth or articles where an invisib finish is required. Use fre machine darning for sma holes or for thin patches o household linen and towels. special fine mending threac obtainable from some sewin machine shops, should be use as ordinary sewing thread pr duces a darn which is to heavy and hard. Remove t foot from the machine ar lower the feed teeth. Make su that the top and bottom te sion are exactly the same. Tri away the ragged edges of t hole, endeavoring to make either circular or oval (th patches do not, of cour require trimming).

Mark two circles around t hole with basting stitches. T inner circle should be $\frac{1}{4}$in aw from the edge of the h and the outer, a $\frac{1}{2}$in away fr the edge. Place the work in embroidery hoop the wr side upward.

The embroidery hoop is h with a hand on each side of frame with the fingers ly just inside the frame. Be v careful to keep the finger away from the needle cause, with the foot off, needle is unprotected.

Lower the pressure foot start the machine, moving frame backward and forw with a regular movement. Work in the direction of weft threads first. Darn b and forth within the sma basted circle. Try not to tate when you change direc at the edge or the darn develop an uneven look.

When the inner outline filled, turn the frame and in a similar way, following warp grain and working wi the outer line of bas The hole should then be and the area around the strengthened.

Darning
leather and suede

First, work close buttonhole stitch all around the hole, working on the right side using a fine needle and a matching thread.

Open-buttonhole stitch is then worked into the edge of the

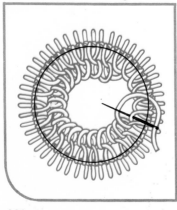

buttonholing, working around and around until the hole is filled.

Splits in leather or suede fabric, such as those which sometimes occur between the fingers of gloves, can be mended by the same method, working along the edges of the split.

Machine darning

Some sewing machines require special attachments, while others have a built-in darning mechanism. If your machine does not have the necessary darning mechanism, and no attachments are available for that type of machine, darning is still possible by working a combined patch and machine darn. Use this type of mending